SIMA FISHER-THE ARTIST

About the Artist/About the Author-SIMA FISHER

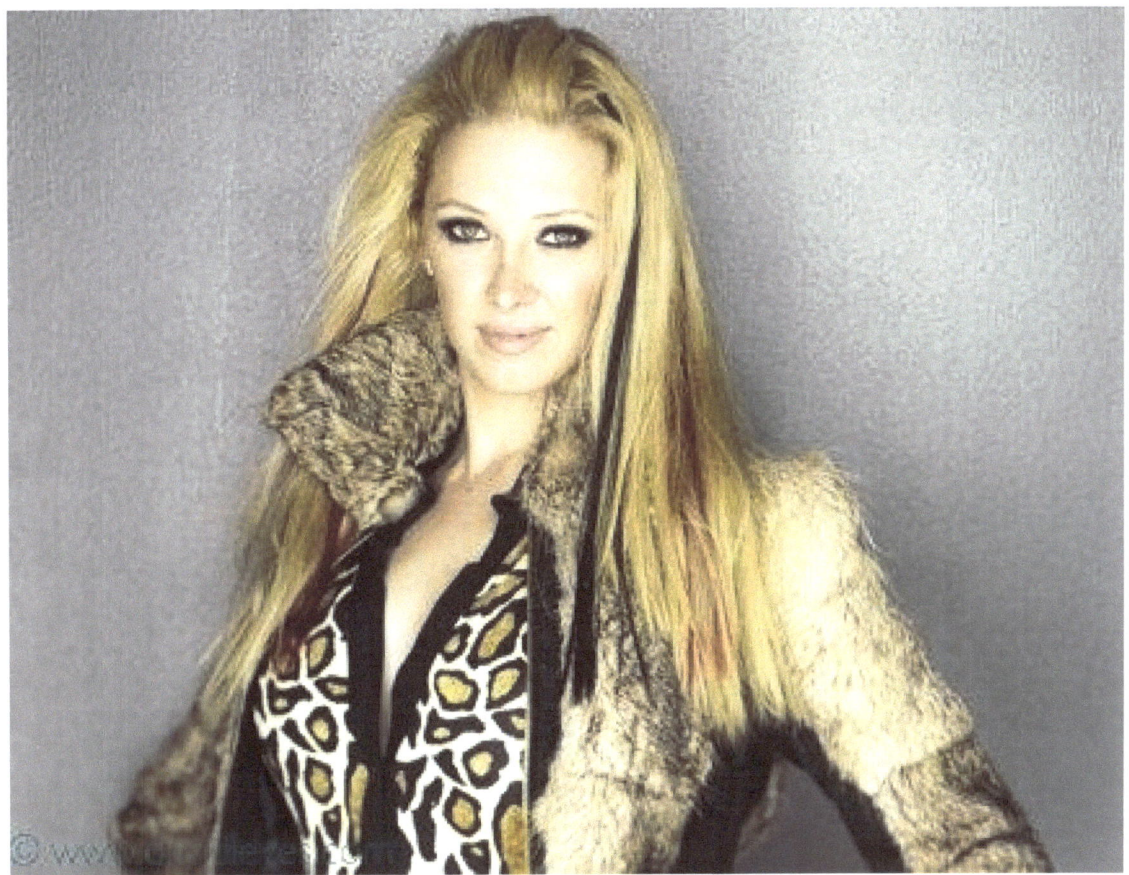

Sima Fisher ARTS.

I wanted to welcome you to my book and websites. I have two main websites www.simafisher.com which is more of a blog about everything creative I've been up to over the years. My other sites www.simafisherarts.com and www.simafisherartgallery.com are strictly visual arts. I love to act, sing, dance, and paint. I get busy with all of my creativity. I was born with that "artistic brain" and I function best when I combine all of my talents together. I Song write, create live shows, have many visual ideas and concepts and have also written some comedy and screenplay. I have created this poetry and art book to display and offer something to you in one book compilation. Hope you enjoy it! LOVE SIM SIMMA!

Sima Fisher a young, multi-talented artist whose career has been gaining strength both internationally and abroad. Her art is very vibrant, colorful and consists of floral, animals and scenery. She uses different sized brushes to get the brush strokes she desires and has recently started to add different textures to her paintings. She works with watercolor, oil and acrylic on canvas. She is a self-taught Impressionism artist who picks up different ideas from artists around her and makes them her own.

Sima's natural ability to create artistic images comes from her spirituality, imagination and child-like freedom of creativity. Sima has also has been featured in many magazines and online publications including Art Tour International which is available in Barnes & Noble's Book store. She continues to be a part of California Art scene displaying her paintings in several locations around L.A.

Her work has been sold to collectors in Toronto, Montreal,Los Angeles, Florida, Michigan, and New York.

Sima works in Acrylic, Oil and multi-medium compositions on canvas.
Today you can see Sima Fisher's work in Wynwood

She enjoys mainstream exposure and critical praise from leaders in the arts, music and acting industries since launching her career twelve years ago. Sima continues to create new series of Art in Artist Alley with the inspiration and motivation of her fellow artists.

Art Gallery Location: Wynwood Miami 46 NW 36st Suite 6, Miami, Florida, 33127

ENCHANTED GARDEN

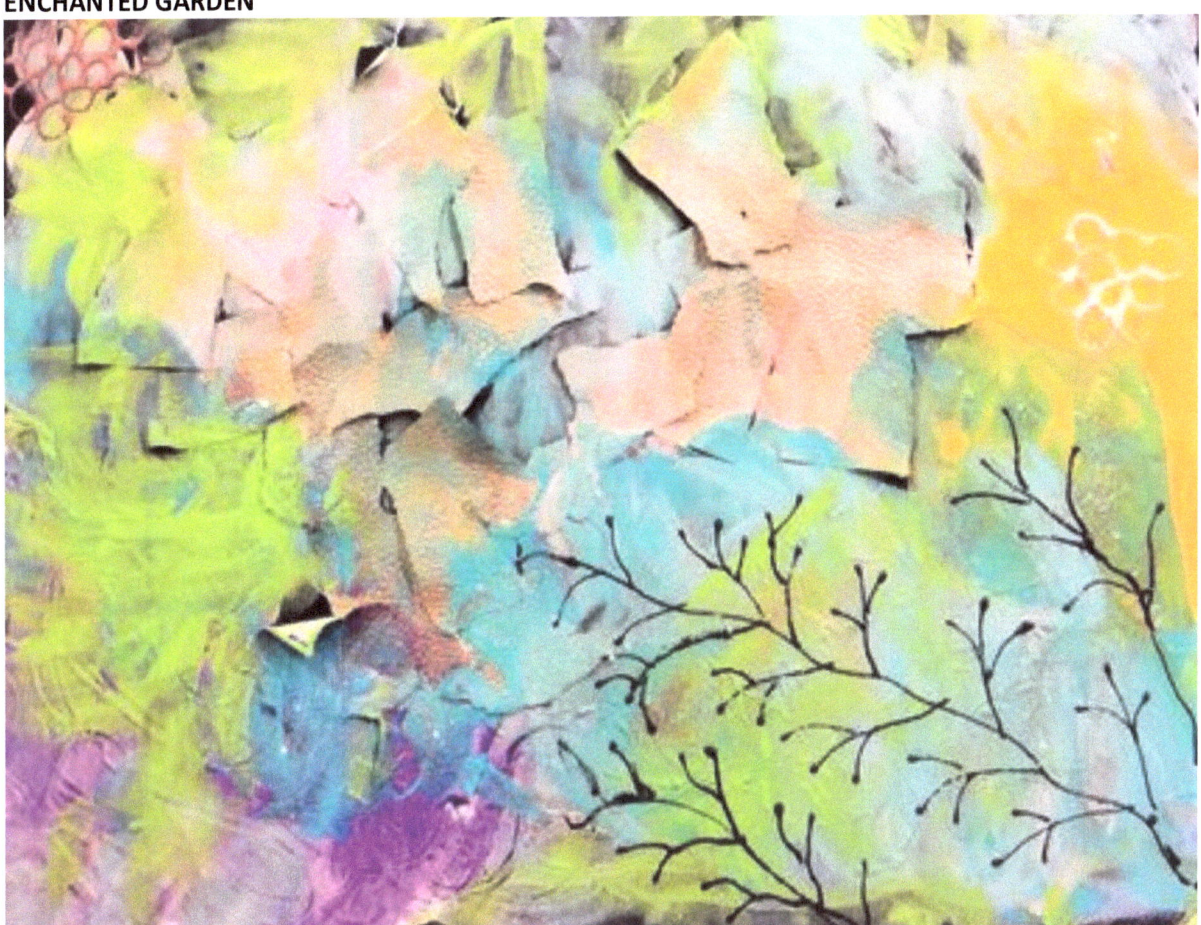

The Enchanted Unweeded Garden is very much a layered and textured painting filled with layers of love and life. It is that unweeded Garden that has all the joys, love, Success, hatred, passion of a relationship.

HORSES IN LOVE

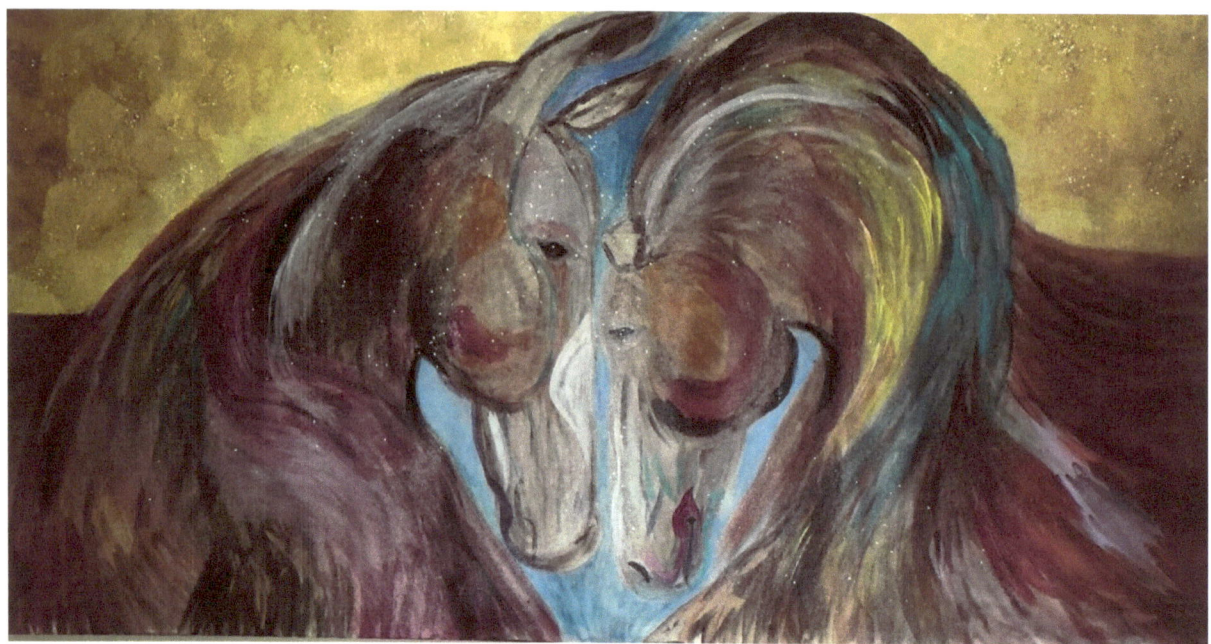

The Passion of these horses coming together, staring into one Another's eyes in a loving and passionate way. The female to the right is dominated by the masculine powers of the male.

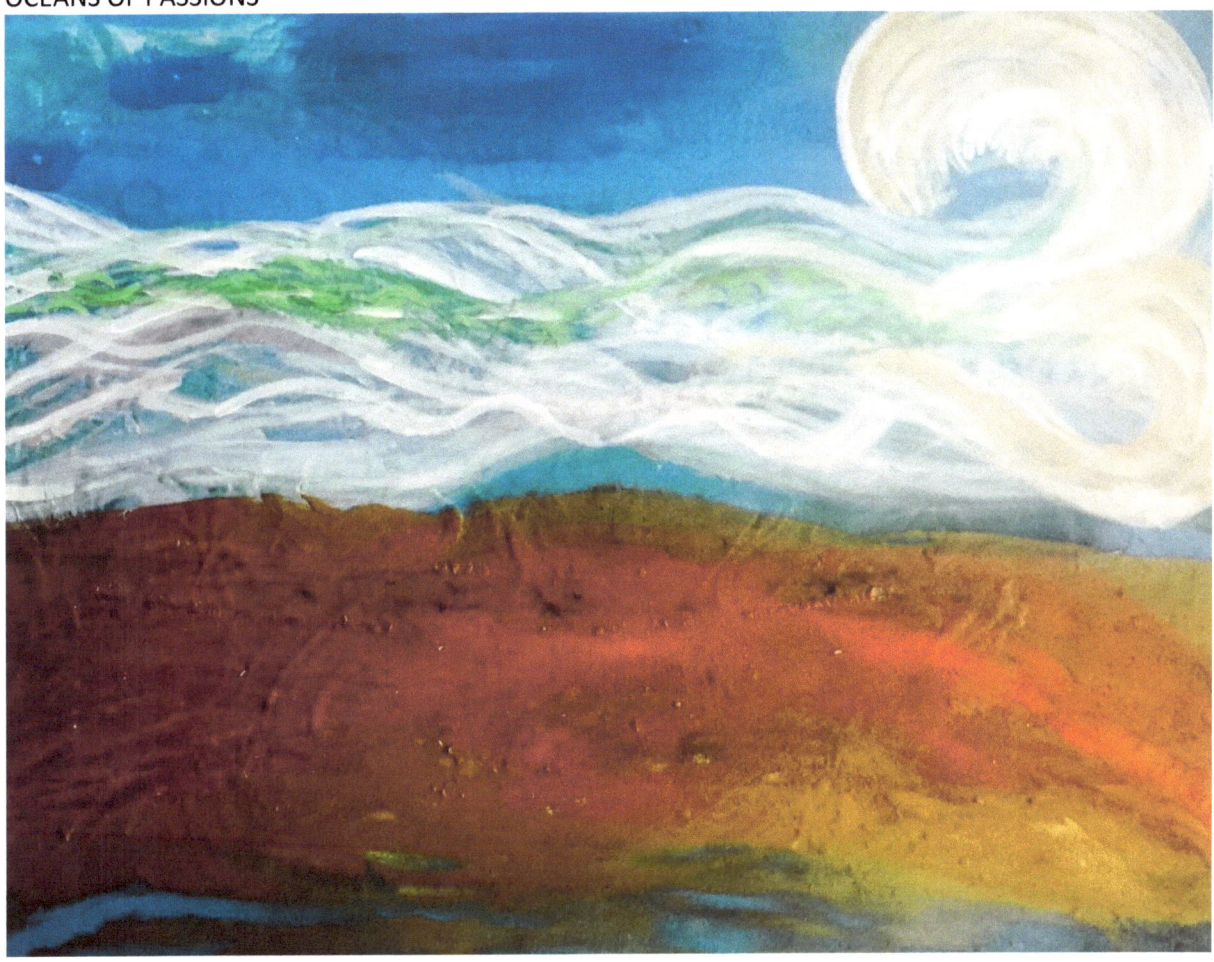

Oceans go by day by day. Every day I wonder where you are. Will you come back to me and stay. I've sent many messages to you over and over and I'm waiting patiently for you to leave her and come back to your family. Although I know they won't let us be together I still want you to come my way.

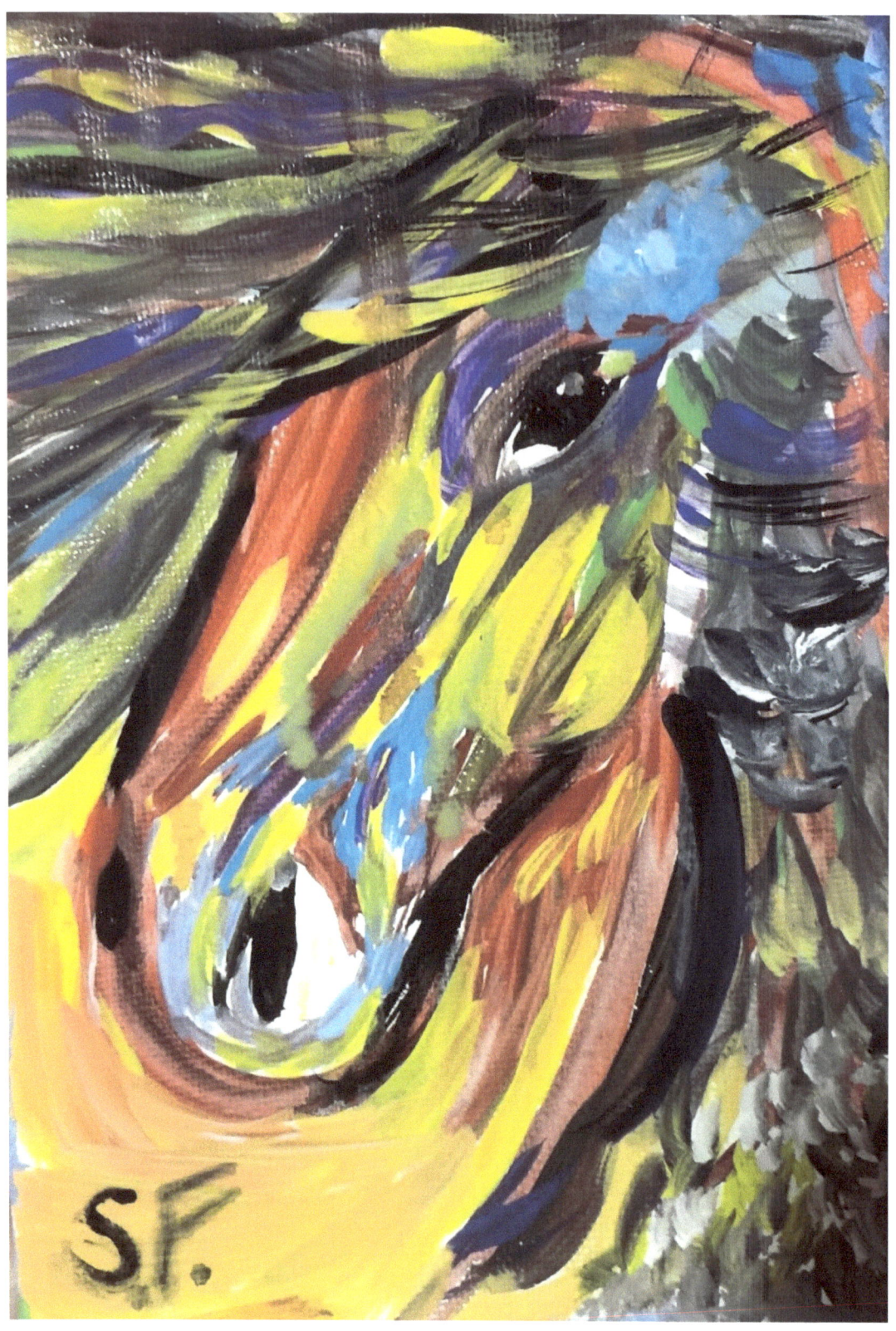

DRIPPING HORSE

THE LUSTFUL OCEAN

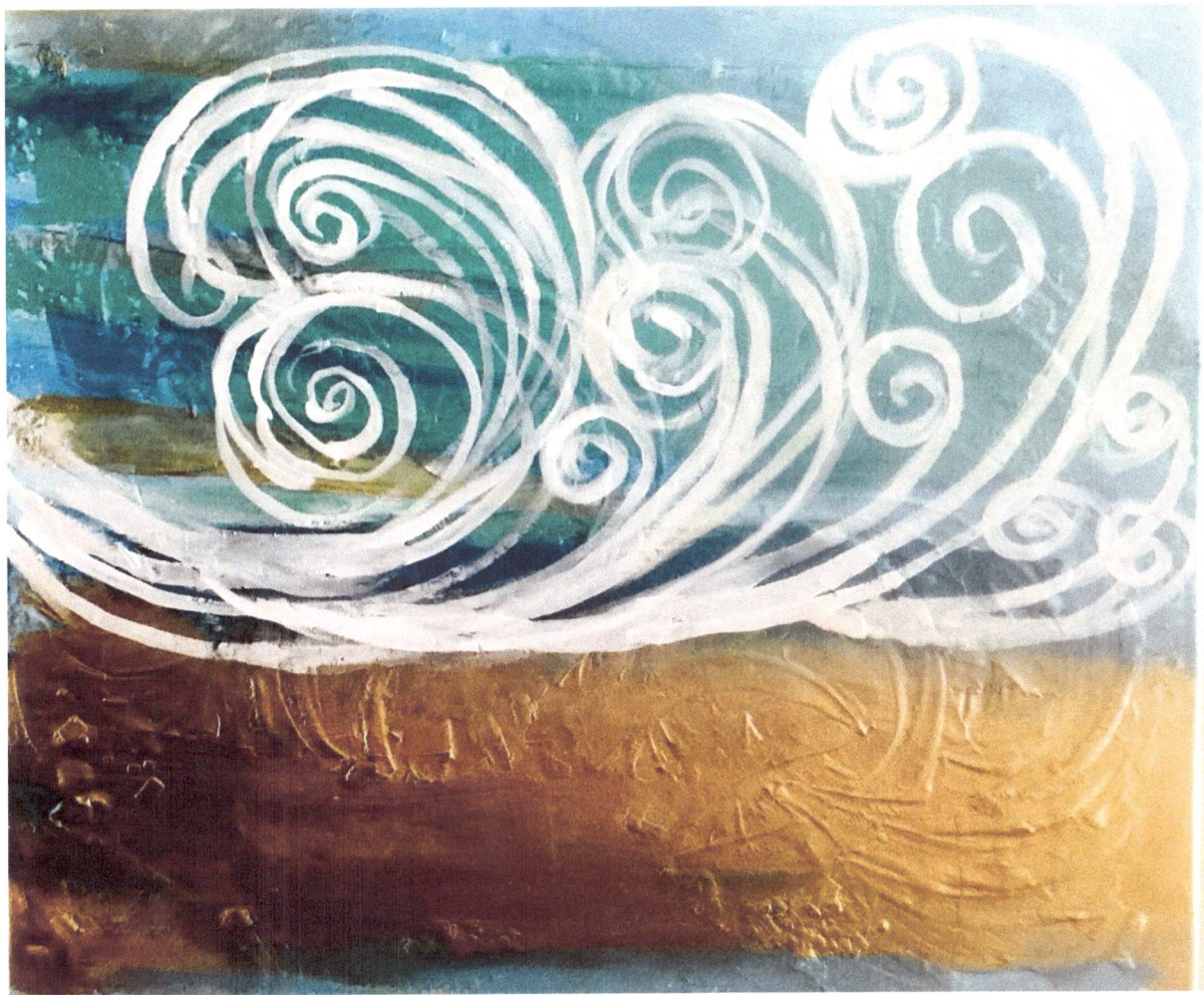

You were attracted to all her bells and whistles. To her fancy bags, to those high heels and the fake job she went to. You got free stuff from her including her passion. I was left behind but I have much more to offer. To the next one who comes along? He will be my hero

PEACOCK FLOWER

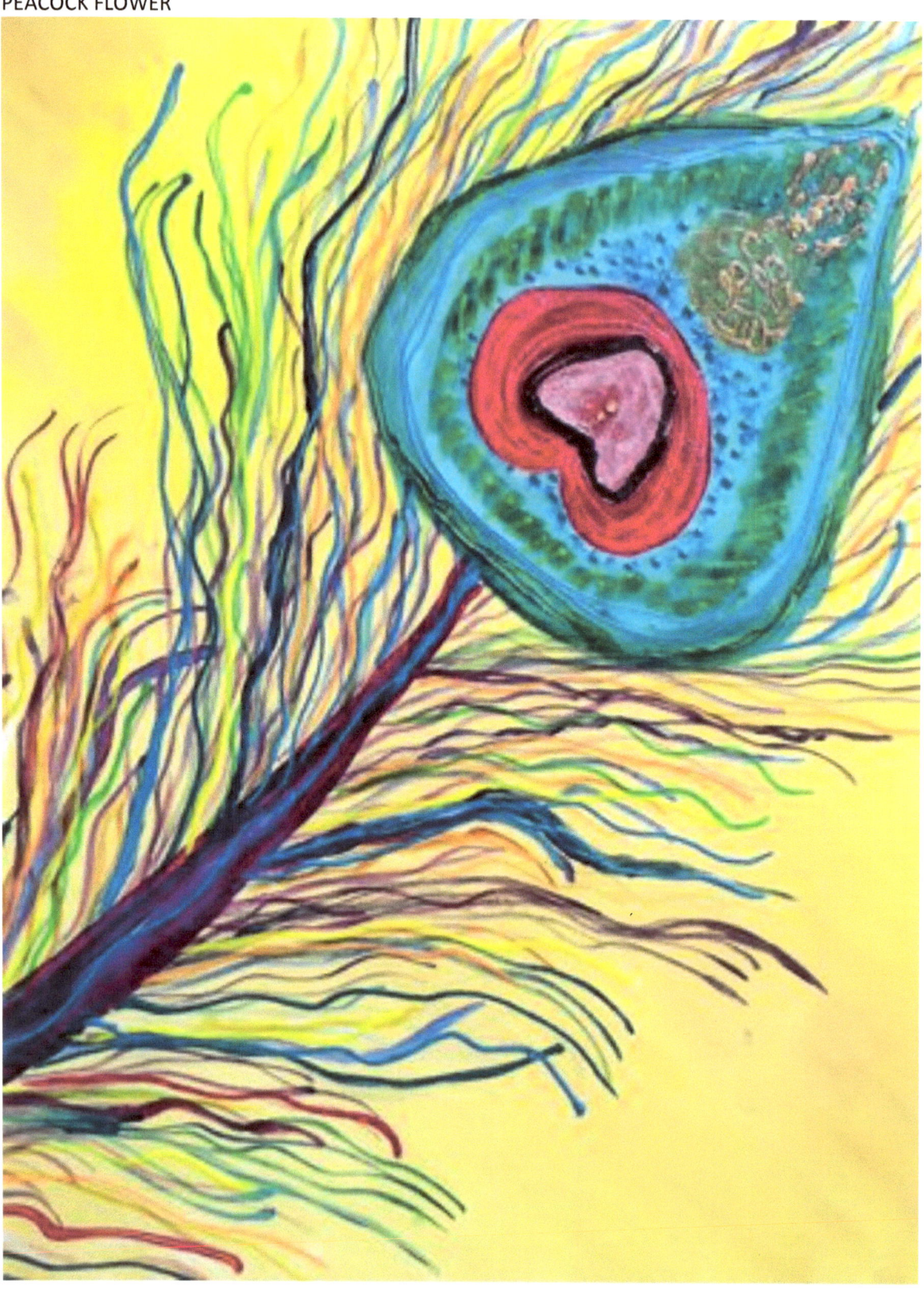

You went to ruffle your feathers in Los Angeles with all the plastic models. Be gone with you now and never look back to me. Just go. Don't look back. Don't look back.

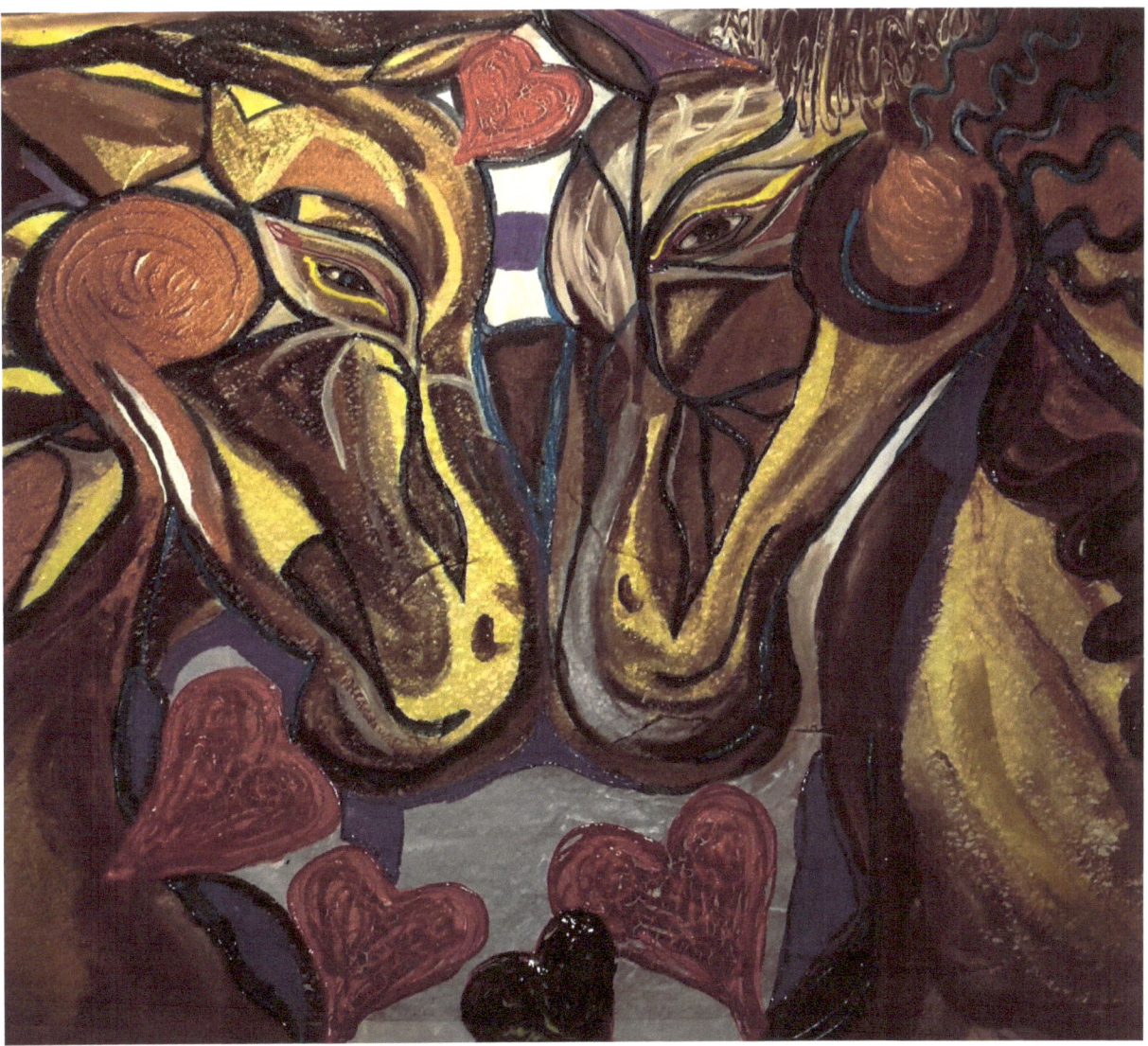

Horses bond and they bond forever. The true love is within me always. I have a blackened heart from all the times we shared that were wrong. But I have three others that replace you. Yes we will butt heads and make up along the way. You are my passion and I'll always walk back your way.

PASSIONATE INDIAN WOMAN

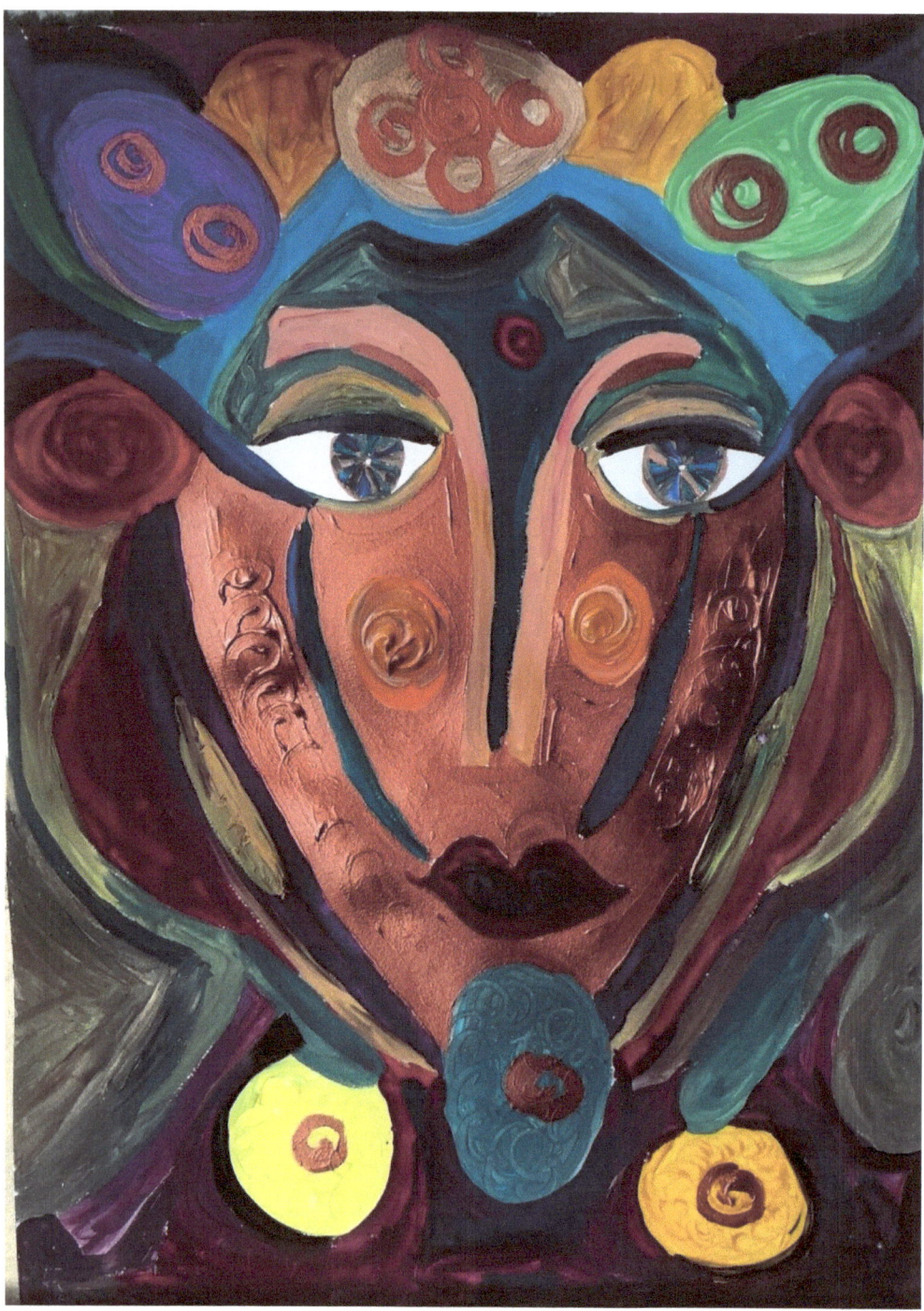

Her intelligence proceeds her. Her passion lives within. She has something to teach me. About friendship and religion.

Crime Scene-By Sima Fisher

You can never see what u are going thru till you remove yourself from the crime scene
My spirit floated out of my own body after it had Been brutally punished, beaten and demeaned
I was reborn again and protected by my angels. All I did was reach up my hand to without opening my
eyes I listened carefully
You made me cry
You told me oh so many lies
But I got away from u
I got away
I got away
I was led astray by some evil force
At the time I thought I was lucky not realizing I got into bed with and warmed up to the devil lawyer
It was a trap that took me awhile to get out of
But I'm never looking back
Never looking back
I got away from u
I'm never looking back

Long Hot Baths-by Sima Fisher

Long HOT Baths

take long hot baths
To prepare for my evening
Of making them all want to rush to take a quick cold shower
It's not my fault
It's not theirs either
It's the modern world we live
Where's the family values
All who get divorced
It's not my fault
It's not there's either
It's not my fault
It's not my fault
It's not my fault
I'm a survivalist
In this corruption

Mourning Doves

When the mourning dove comes
he visits to give you faith
to know that it will work out the way it supposed to
people may not always be Godly
he may not always return home
He may fall into his own demons
but you must have faith to do what right
for the mourning dove is with you
the mourning dove is with you

He comes to visit not for food
he comes to deliver a message from God
to have faith
to have faith
when the mourning dove comes to visit

RAINBOW PASSION

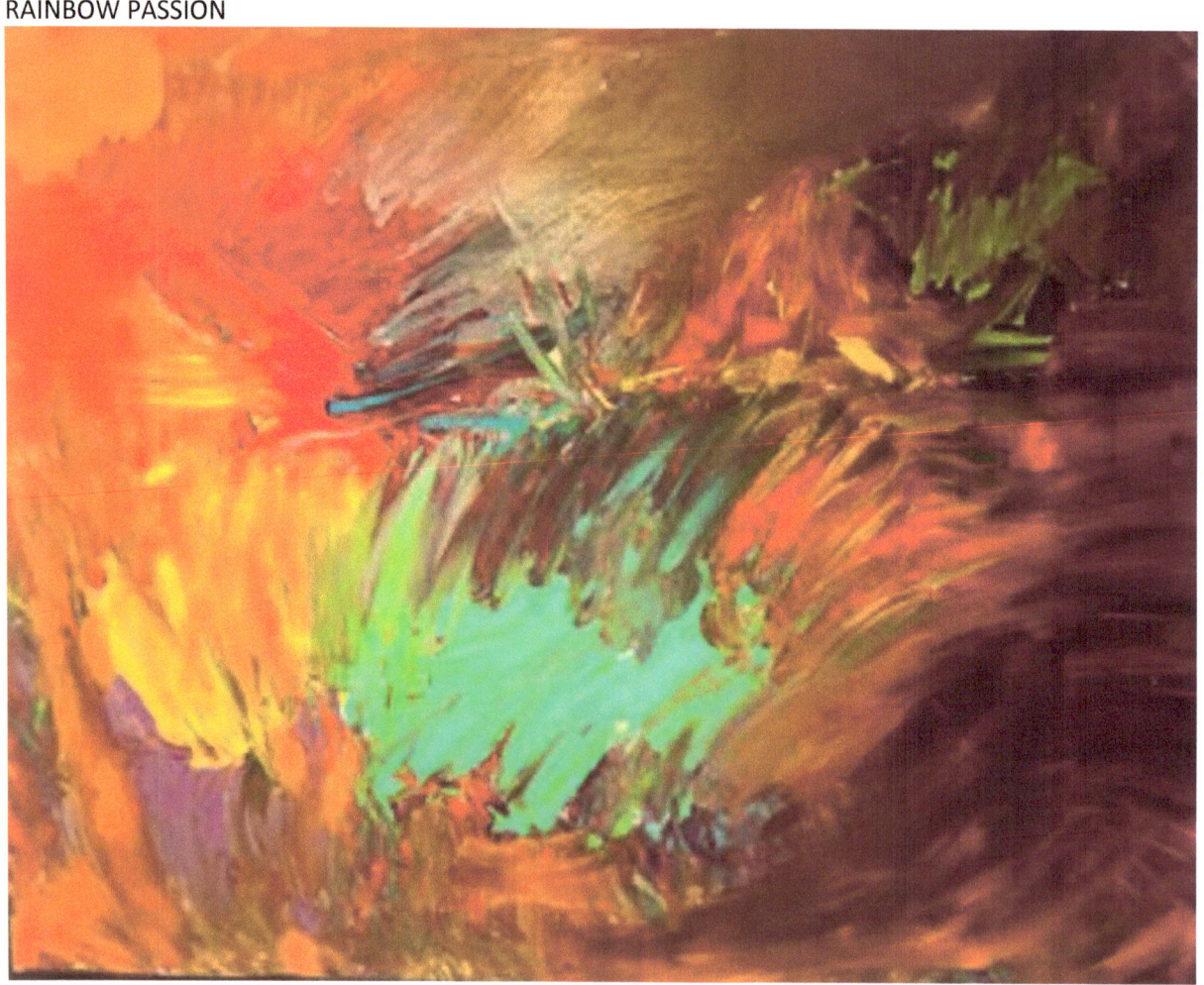

SUNFLOWER GARDEN

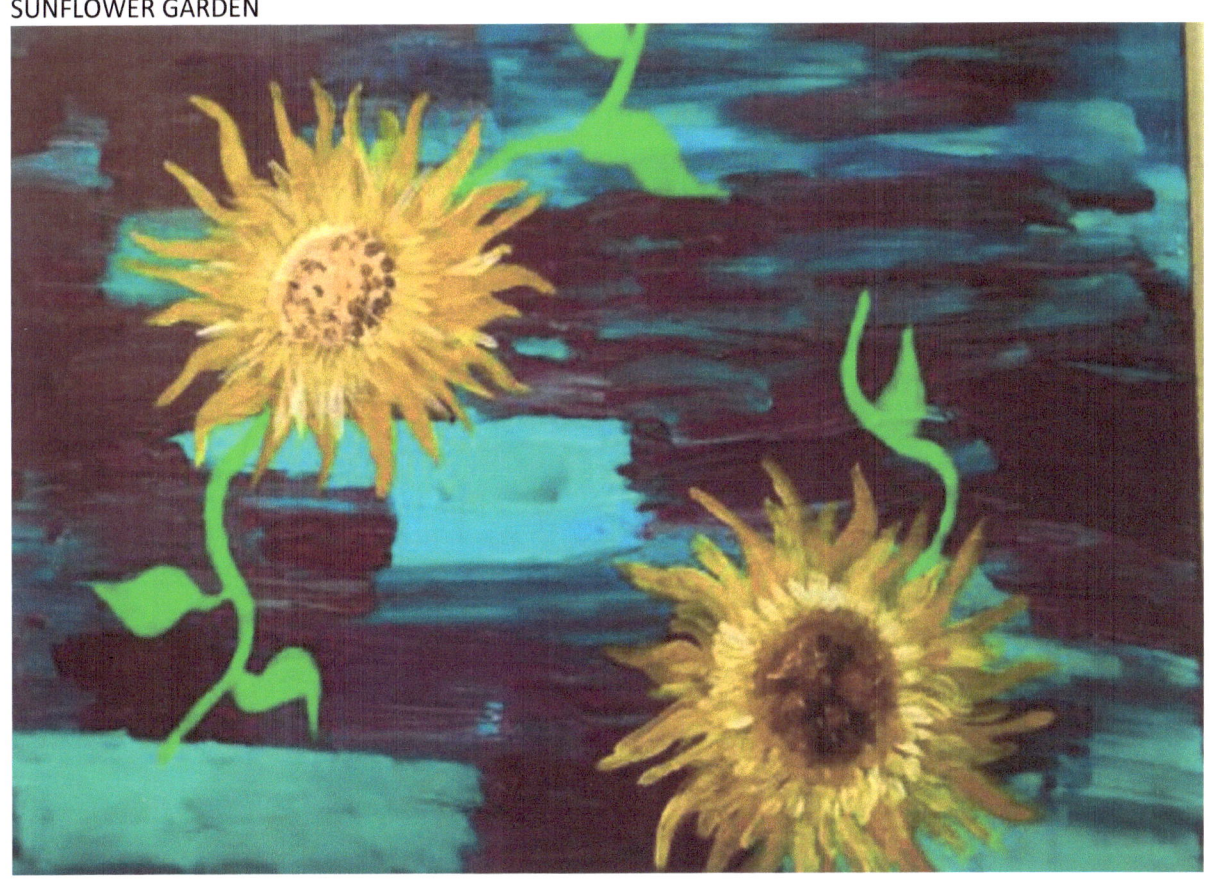

PUFFY TREE

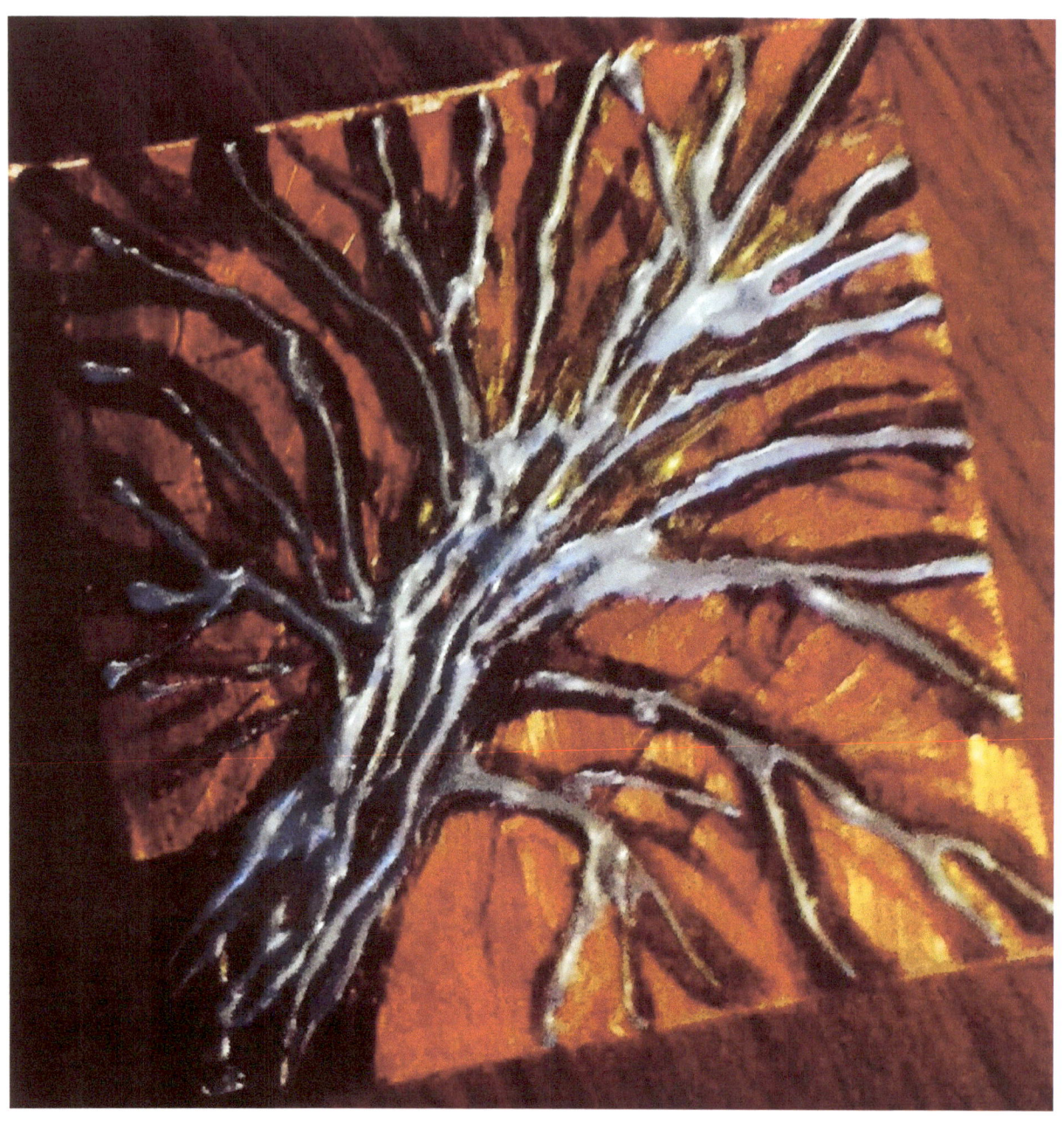

PUFFY TREE 2

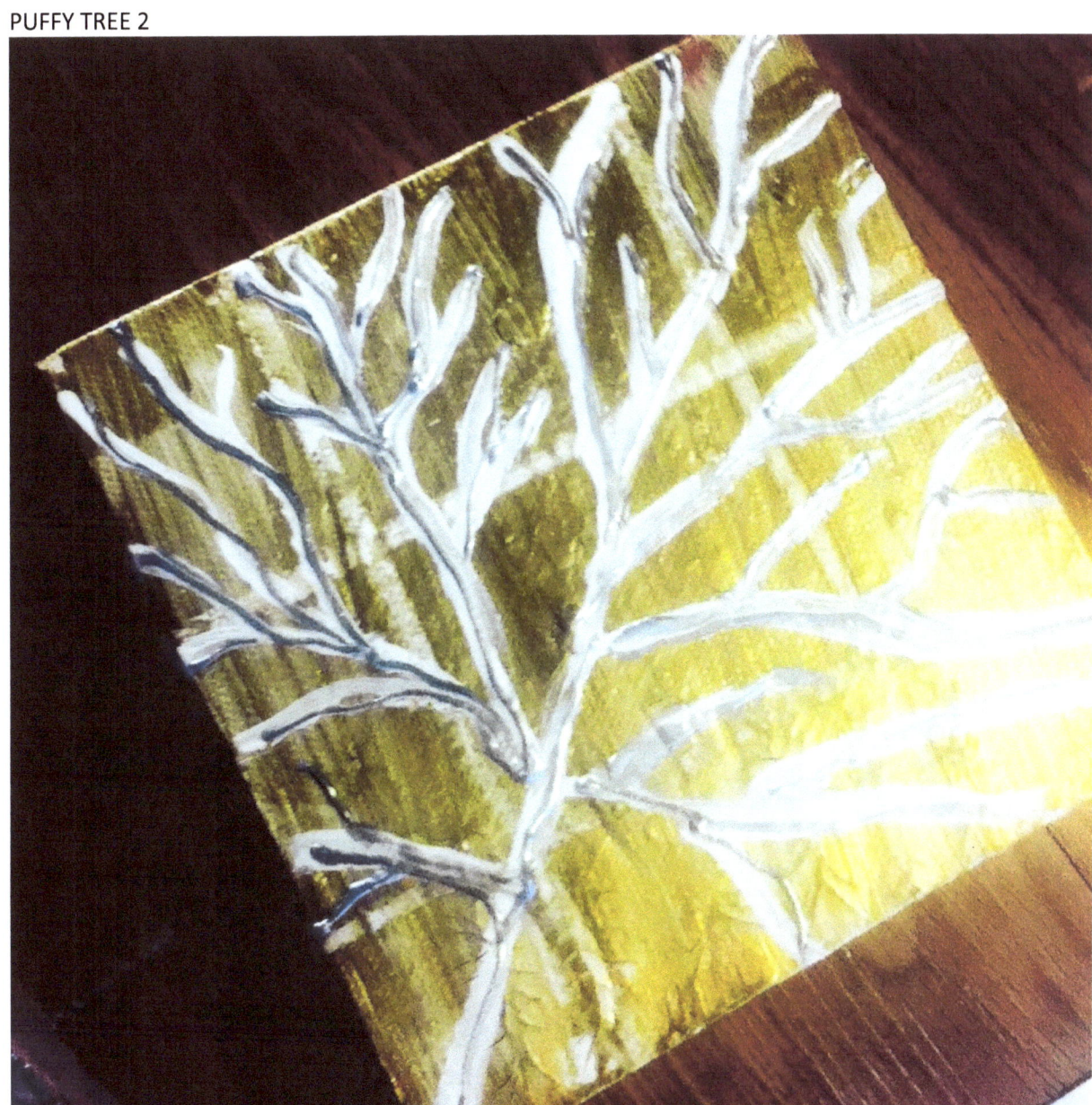

PASSION OF JANET

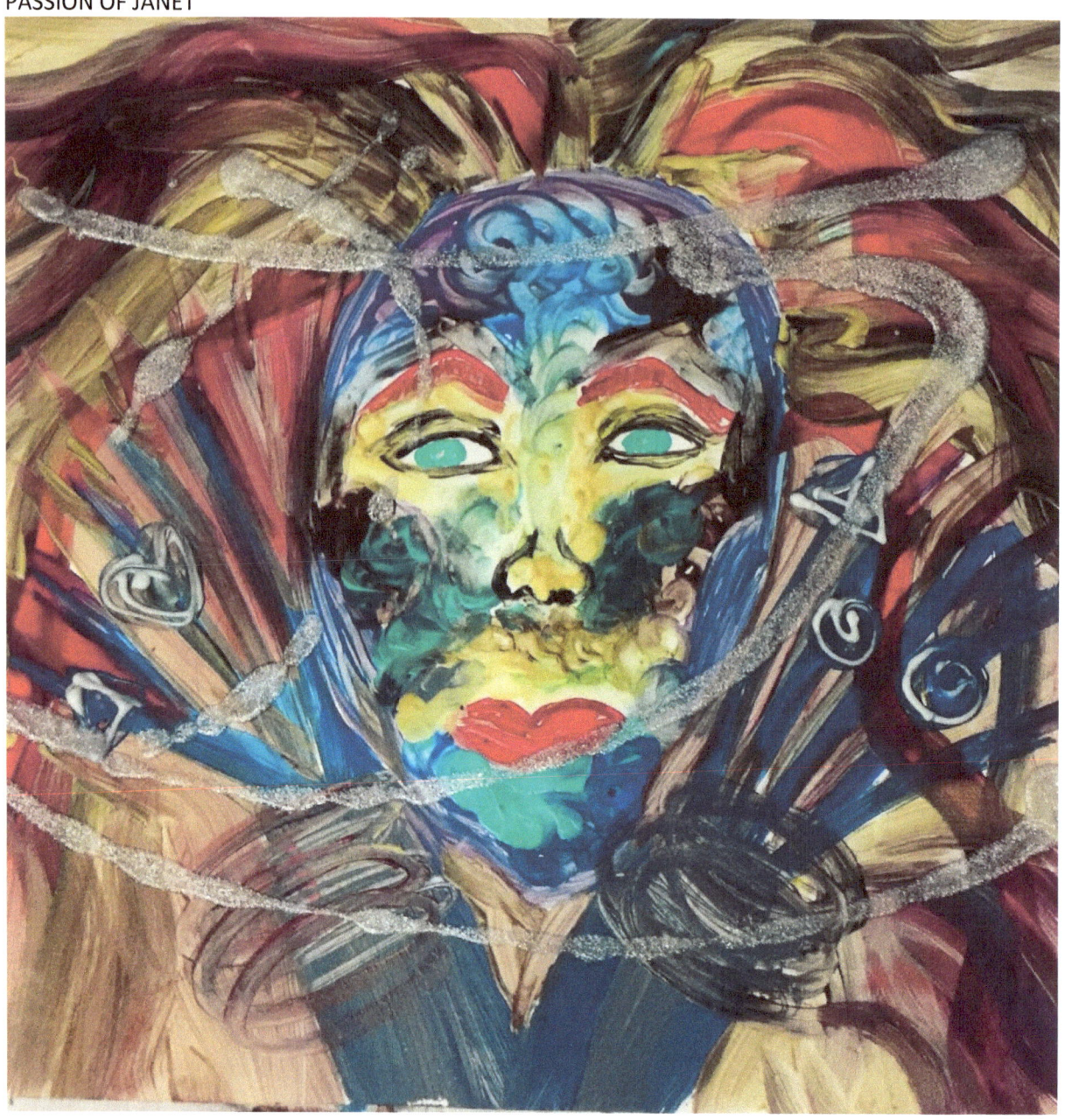

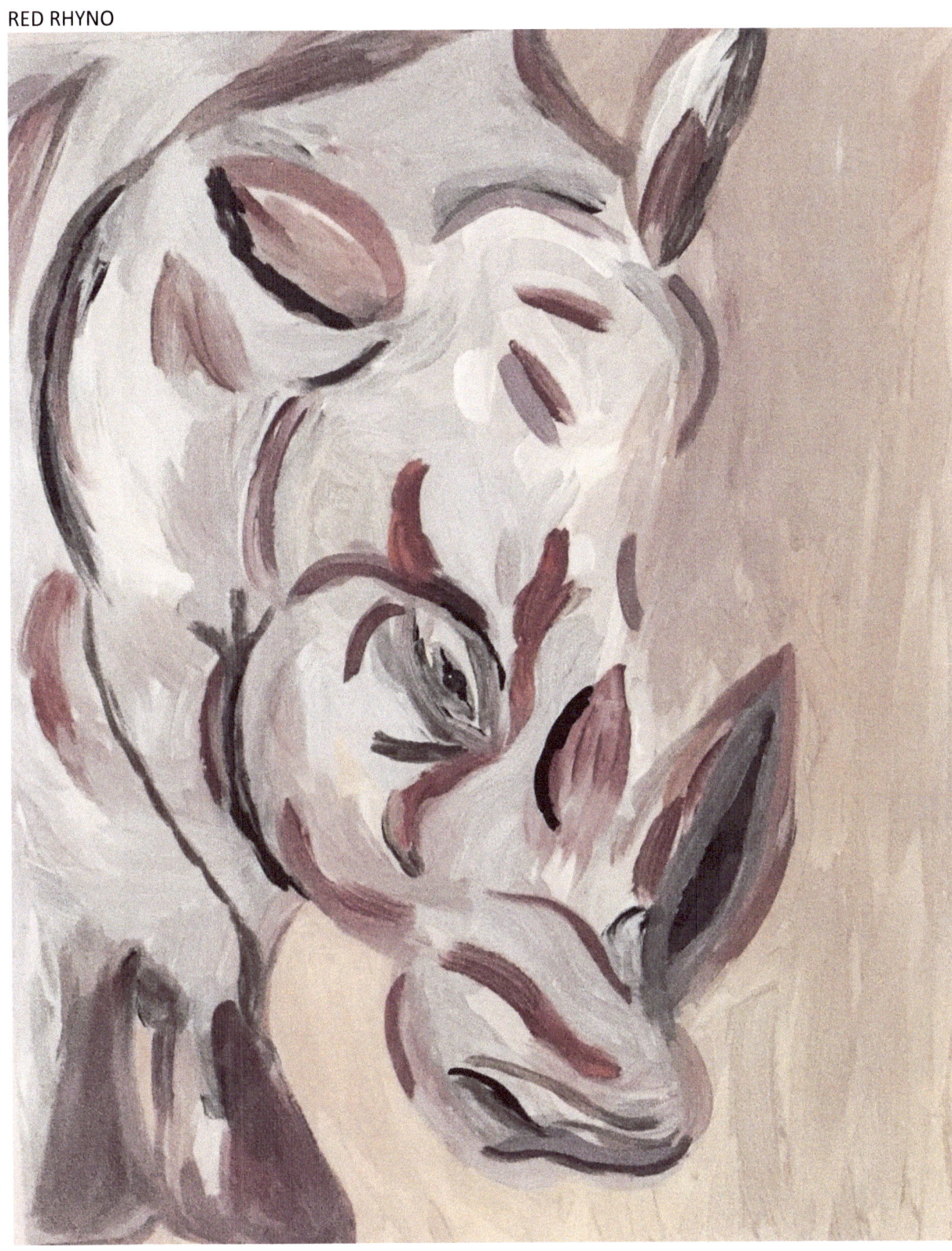

BROWN BUTTERFLY

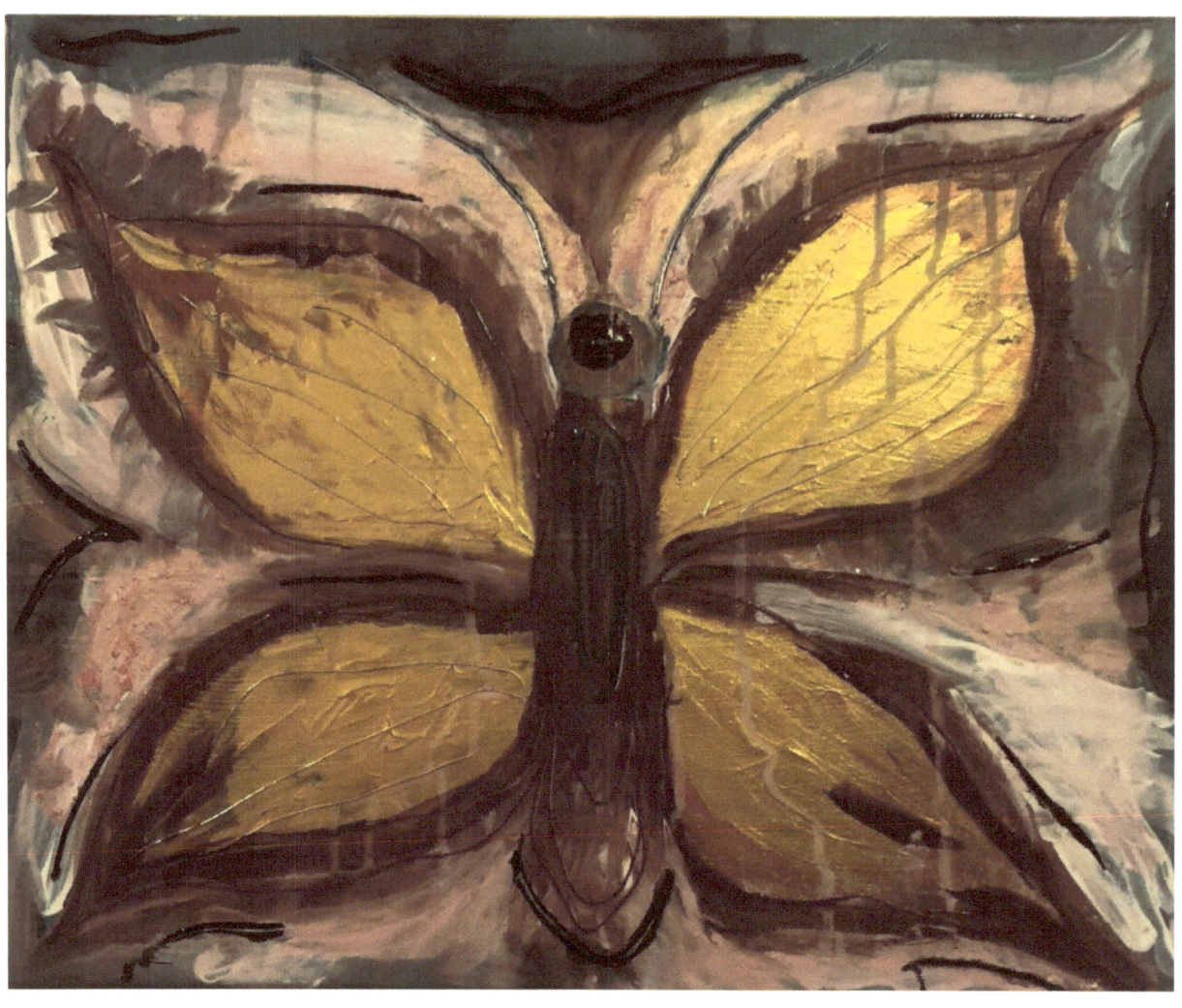

SUNSET TREE

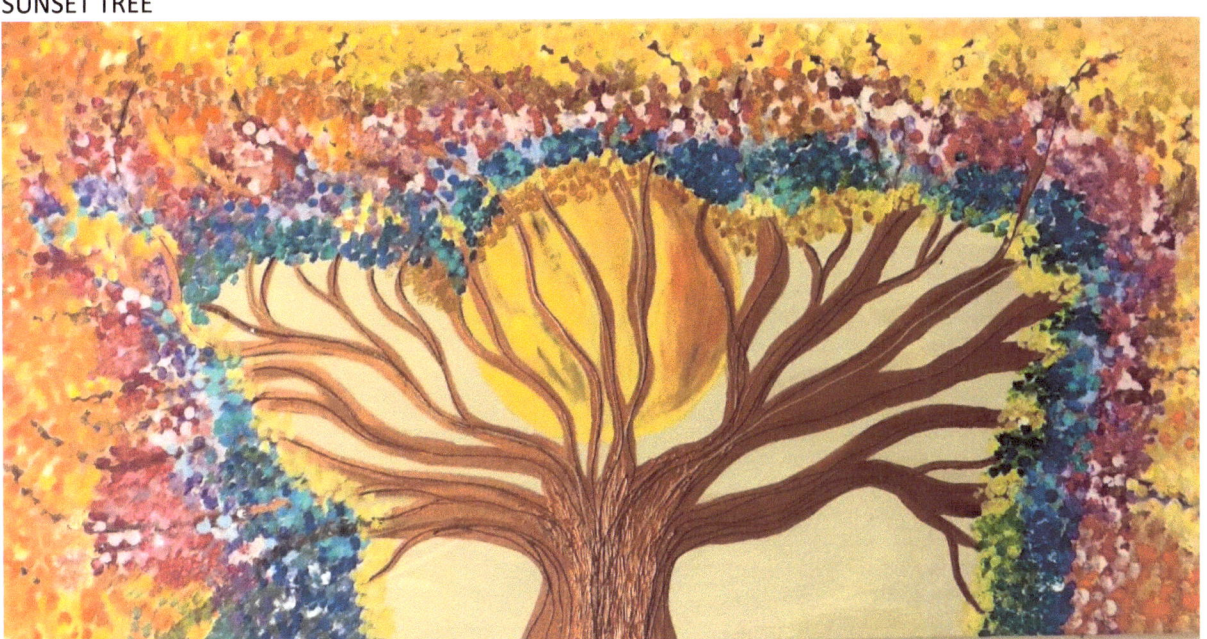

Ages of my life stages of my life poem
When I was:
20 I travelled and worked
30s baby and worked
40s 2nd baby and worked
50s studied more and changed jobs
60s work as a doctor children
70s children and grandchildren
80 grand children
90 grandchildren
100 grand children
These are the stages of my life. Seems so simple yet it's all so complex
Seems like I'd sleep enough and get enough rest
I know every day I'll be put to the test
But I'll survive to see my great grand kids grow up
I'll enjoy myself enough and party but rest

Paths (song)

You were 14 in the hood playing ball with all the future star athletes.
I was playing in my small town too
You were 16 rapping over some tracks that were meant to be seen you had big dreams
I was in my small town dreaming of it too
I had to get outta that town
You needed out of that city too
We both needed a way out
We both did what it took to be strong and shake those people off our feet
And we did
And we did
And we did
We got outta there because we knew there was so much more to life than this

Forever (song)

I'm sitting here thinking about you
All the times we shared came true
We had so many good ones too
A few bumps along the way
I really don't even care what they say
You I know it's true

Not when I'm witchu
I got whatchu want
U got what I want

You make me want forever
You make me feel forever
All I can think is ever
It's you and me in this together forever
Oh yah

It the kind of love that makes me want to be with you
Forever ohhh ohh

All of those times they told me
What I do I care they don't know

Sat up and waited all night
For everything to turn out right

Other woman (song)

There will always be another woman
Always will be
Always was
But you must ask that woman
"What do you want?"
And whatever her reply is you just say
"Move along now"
Like Evita did
Like every Queen does
She grabs ahold of her king
And that's all there is to it
It's called Womanhood"

Who's the one (song)
Who's the one u saw on your IG
Who's the one they all seem to gawk at
Who's the one you all want to talk to
Who's the one who's the one who's the one?

Who's the one you were holding hands with?
Who's the one you stand next to?
I'm the one I'm the one I'm the one

Pain (song)
Don't live with pain and mystery in your heart
Gotta learn to let it go
Cause we won't be here for too long
And you can't have that energy with you in your new start

I've lost who I am (song)
And they all do it to me over and over again

I collect $ from them to make up for the pain
Because I know I'll never be the same

Compensation for all the ugliness bestowed upon me
All that happens is I get used over and over again which divides me

Money doesn't make up for all my pain
I know I'll never be the same

Choices (song)

I've made the wrong choices in life and now I see the consequences
I didn't think about my future to the end and now I suffer greatly
All I do is drink coffee to stay alive
They all warned me what my future would hold
And it's all unfolding in front of me now
All I do is hang onto good moments and try to allow them to make up for all the bad
I cope every day in misery
I can't get away

Heaven send (song)

I threw all my pain into the ocean
And it washed it all away
All my tears wore away
Got swept away
I threw it all into the ocean
I threw all my pain away
I asked why

Why

Why is my life being threatened?
Why am I stuck here?
Is this a lesson of life?
Lessons are taught till learned
Lessons are taught till learned

Stillness (song)

In stillness we find the answers
God grants them in prayer
All you can do is your very best
And go on
Move on

Maybe (song)

Maybe the dishes aren't always clean and out of the sink
Maybe sometime we both have morning breath and we stink
Maybe we nitpick and call each other names like dough bag and whore
Maybe you aren't always careful about locking the front door
But truth be told we can yell till we are black and blue
Truth is I'll get drunk and yell at you all night
Truth is that we will always fuss and fight
And at the end of the day we both stand up and fight
There's no more running away
Even though we may feel betrayed
At the end of the day we love each other in our own little ways

Emotions (songs)

I'm so filled with so many emotions about you
That I never know what to do with them all
They all come out all wrong
All wrong all wrong
They all come out all wrong from so many different levels of wrong
I want to tell you I love you
But I don't want to feel so vulnerable
So instead I slap you with mean words to break you down
So much animosity and pain
I was to take a knife to all your clothes just so you will love me more
It's not healthy I know

I used to (rap songs)

I used to hang out with bad guys who only broke my heart
I used to fuck random dudes who paid my rent
I used to let guys touch me for $20 per song
I was never clever
I let them all do random stuff to me
My daddy died when I was 3
My mommy did her best to raise me straight
She had 8 kids and work with inmates
It isn't my fault she said to me
It ain't your fault
I said it's not your fault either mom
You played with the cards you were dealt the best you could

When my baby boy was 2 months old they took him away from my breast
They gave him to some black lady living in the hood
They told me you can only see him for two hours because you isn't no good
You danced on the pole and showed yourself to all these men
You chose a daddy who beats up women
I bet he beats you too
So I gave them the information they wanted me to
I had to get my baby back
The father of my baby said "it may not be mine"
He took off, he gave up.. He didn't want to ruin his chances at fame with "the game"
I thought he didn't care
So I became strong
I had to take care of my baby boy
But I didn't want my boy to grow up when they no dad
I sacrificed
I was so sad

Free (song)
As a bird
Flying high up in the sky
Free as a bird
Flying so lucky to be so free
Going so fast in a speed boat
They chase us for some food
Imagine the freedom to be a bird

True gem
Diamonds are shaped with pressure
And pearls are made deep down in the ocean over many years of water flowing over them
But you need to know something
You need to know who I am
I'm an opal
I'm taaffeite
I'm red diamonds
I'm the rarest kind you'll ever find
Shitting on me won't work
I can still get cleaned off

Break me down (sculpture) song

You can try try try to break me down
You can chip away at me like a sculpture
You can emotionally abuse me because you think nobody will notice.
But they all see the pain in my eyes
They all see right through your lies.
You could try to turn our child against me
You can keep trying because it's not gonna ever work
I'm too strong
Pressure makes diamonds

I was under a pile of garbage and he plucked me out of it and told me I'm worth so much more than you
Because all you do is pretend it Public that you love me
Than abuse me
All this pretending is embarrassing because everyone sees through it all

Ages of my life stages of my life poem
When I was:
20 I travelled and worked
30s baby and worked
40s 2nd baby and worked
50s studied more and changed jobs
60s work as a doctor children
70s children and grand children
80 grand children
90 grandchildren
100 grand children
These are the stages of my life. Seems so simple yet it's all so complex
Seems like I'd sleep enough and get enough rest
I know every day I'll be put to the test
But I'll survive to see my great grand kids grow up
I'll enjoy myself enough and party but rest

Paths (song)

You were 14 in the hood playing ball with all the future star athletes.
I was playing in my small town too
You were 16 rapping over some tracks that were meant to be seen you had big dreams
I was in my small town dreaming of it too

I had to get outta that town
You needed out of that city too
We both needed a way out
We both did what it took to be strong and shake those people off our feet
And we did
And we did
And we did
We got outta there because we knew there was so much more to life than this

Forever (song)

I'm sitting here thinking bout you
All the times we shared came true
We had so many good ones too
A few bumps along the way
I really don't even care what they say
You I know it's true

Not when I'm witchu
I got whatchu want
U got what I want

You make me me want forever
You make me feel forever
All I can think is ever
It's you and me in this together forever
Oh yah

It the kind of love that makes me want to be with you
Forever ohhh ohh

All of those times they told me
What I do I care they don't know

Sat up and waited all night
For everything to turn out right

Without your love-song

Without your love my rosé petals wilt
They die in the darkness of my guilt

Without your love there's only me and me alone
And the baby you gave me is all I need now

For I am stubborn and will never give in
I will never let you close again

Without your love they can try to take but I cannot give

You left us here to seek out darkness

In survival mode was your only way

Since you could only drown me I had to kick you off of me.
I can't look back to you now
You have to find your own ship

Just in case (are u still strong enough to be my man)
You decide to leave me
He's been watching me pose on Instagram
Just in case
My Facebook status gets set to "single"
Just in case you think that girl is better than me
Oh no no no, there is the door
I know you found her on your Instagram and many more before
And invited her to your basketball game
Then when she got there she wasn't so good
You being so lame
So Just in case, I have him all lined up.
Just in case
I know there's life out there after you
I'll leave that door always open for you to leave

You really you think you can away with that
It's amusing to me
That you think I believe your lies.
I see through them however
I'll let you wear your disguise.
For the truth is too much
For you to reveal
I know it has nothing to do with
Me how you feel

I noticed that you've changed
Something's different about you
By Sima Fisher

Hurricane (song)

You burst through your pathway like a hurricane knocking down everything in your path
But you can't knock down this stable tree because my roots are deep down witting the solid soil
for years and years of growth. Like the tree at the museum that's is over 1400 years old. I'm solid
and not going nowhere so you better get used to me. Maybe you are physically stronger than me
but I'm solid like a peach

You're not like the others (song)
That's why you won my love
You convinced me for sure
It's the fine balance of what people want from you
And what you are willing to give up
I know it too well
I know it all too well

Those lips (song)
Those lips I've kissed a million times
Yet I never really could feel you completely till now
All the layers I've uncovered
All the years revealed
The trueness that you are to me
The completeness that you've given to me
I'll be willing to give myself fully to you now
I'm able to do it now
I can do it without flinching
I can do it because you are with me

Oh wow (song)
You want to stay out all night
Searching for women who want to get it right
That's ok go do your thing
I'm gonna get mine too
Since I'm here stuck with you
What other choice do I have?
But to get myself distracted

Who's the one (song)
Who's the one u saw on your IG
Who's the one they all seem to gawk at
Who's the one you all want to talk to
Who's the one who's the one who's the one?

Who's the one you were holding hands with Who's the one you stand next to
I'm the one I'm the one I'm the one

STRANGE LADY

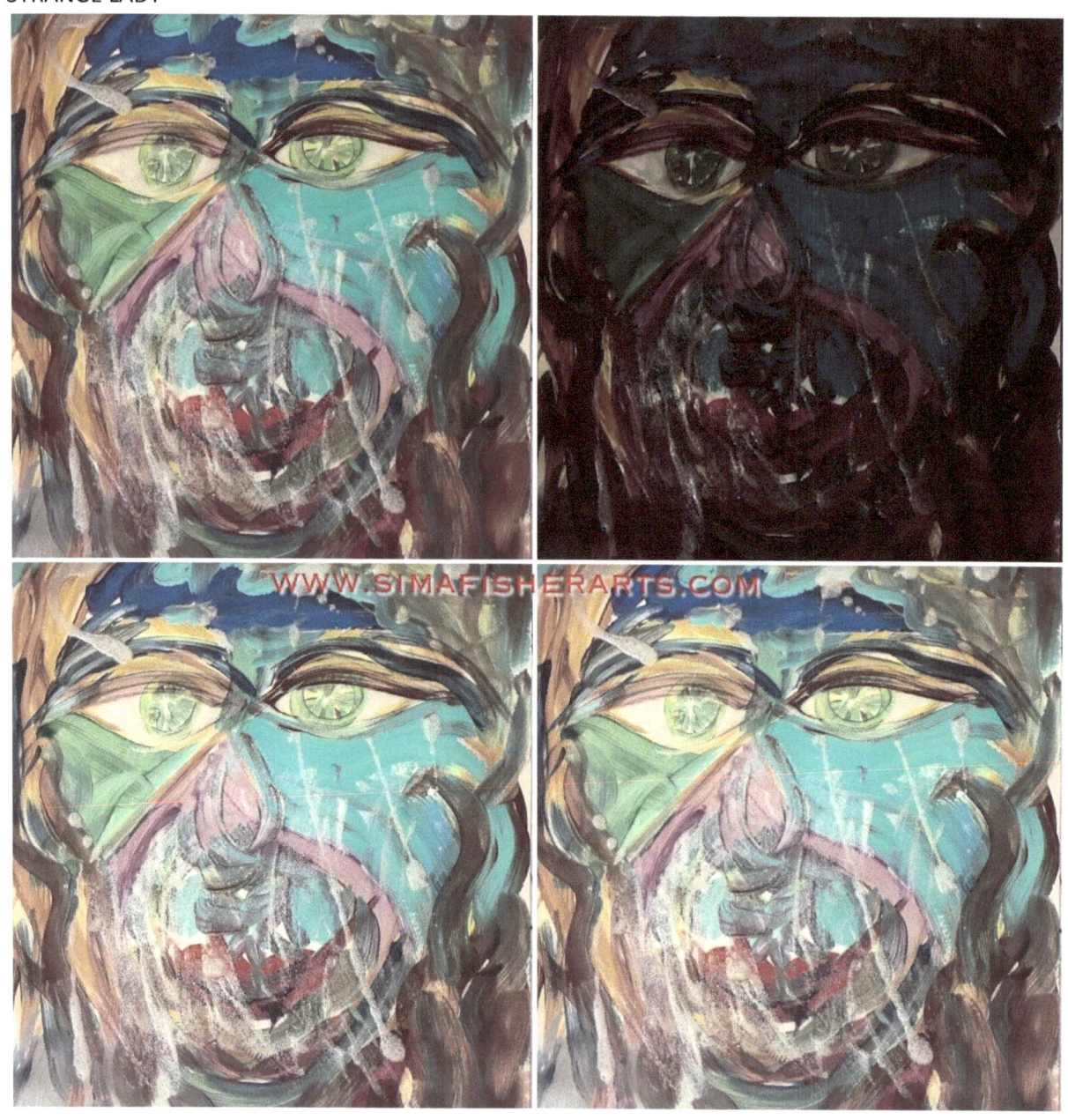

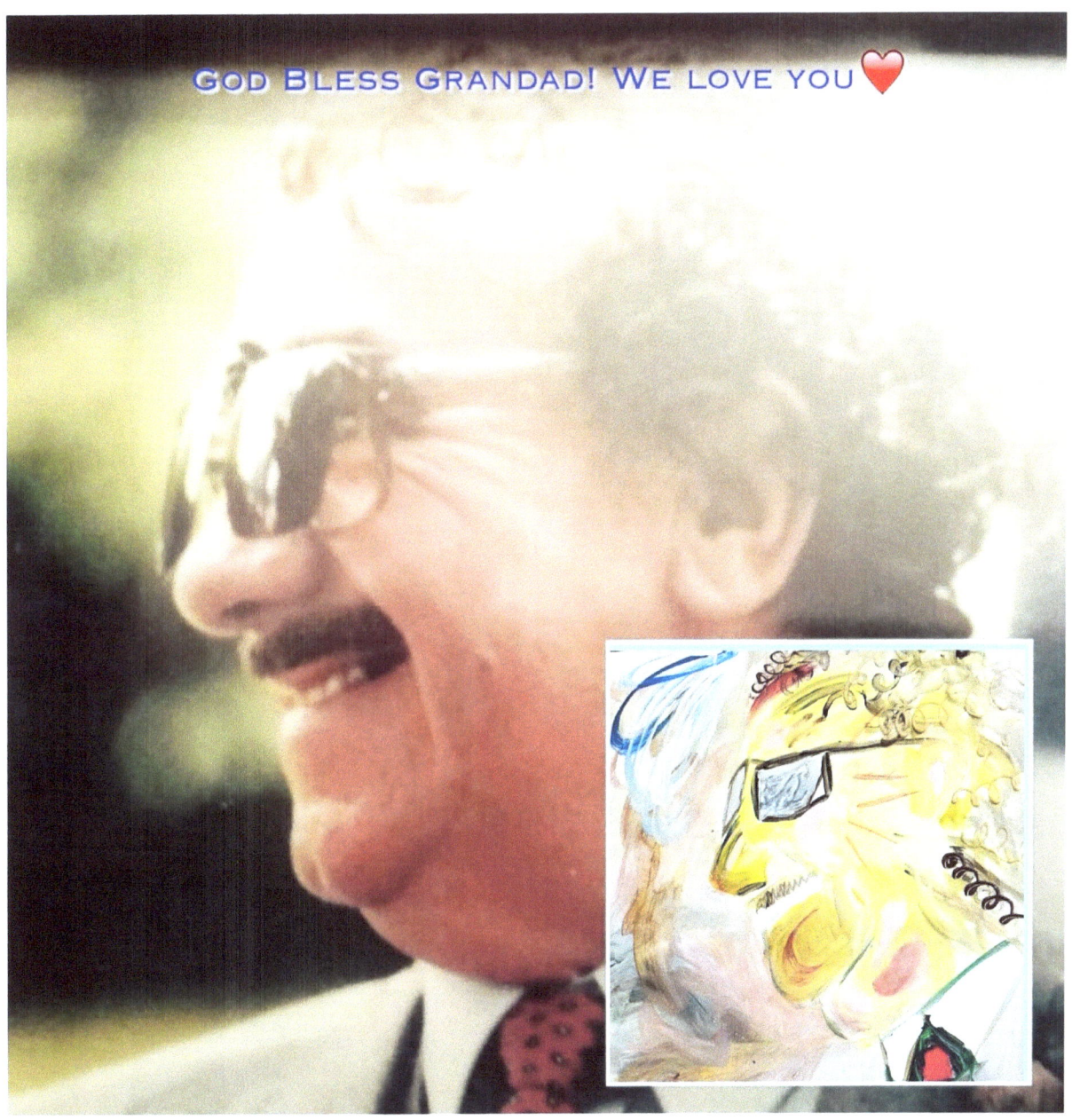

GOD BLESS GRANDAD! WE LOVE YOU ❤️

We Love You Granddad. You left this world but you are waiting for us in a new happier place. You are most likely having a drink of two with my father. You are in our thoughts daily.

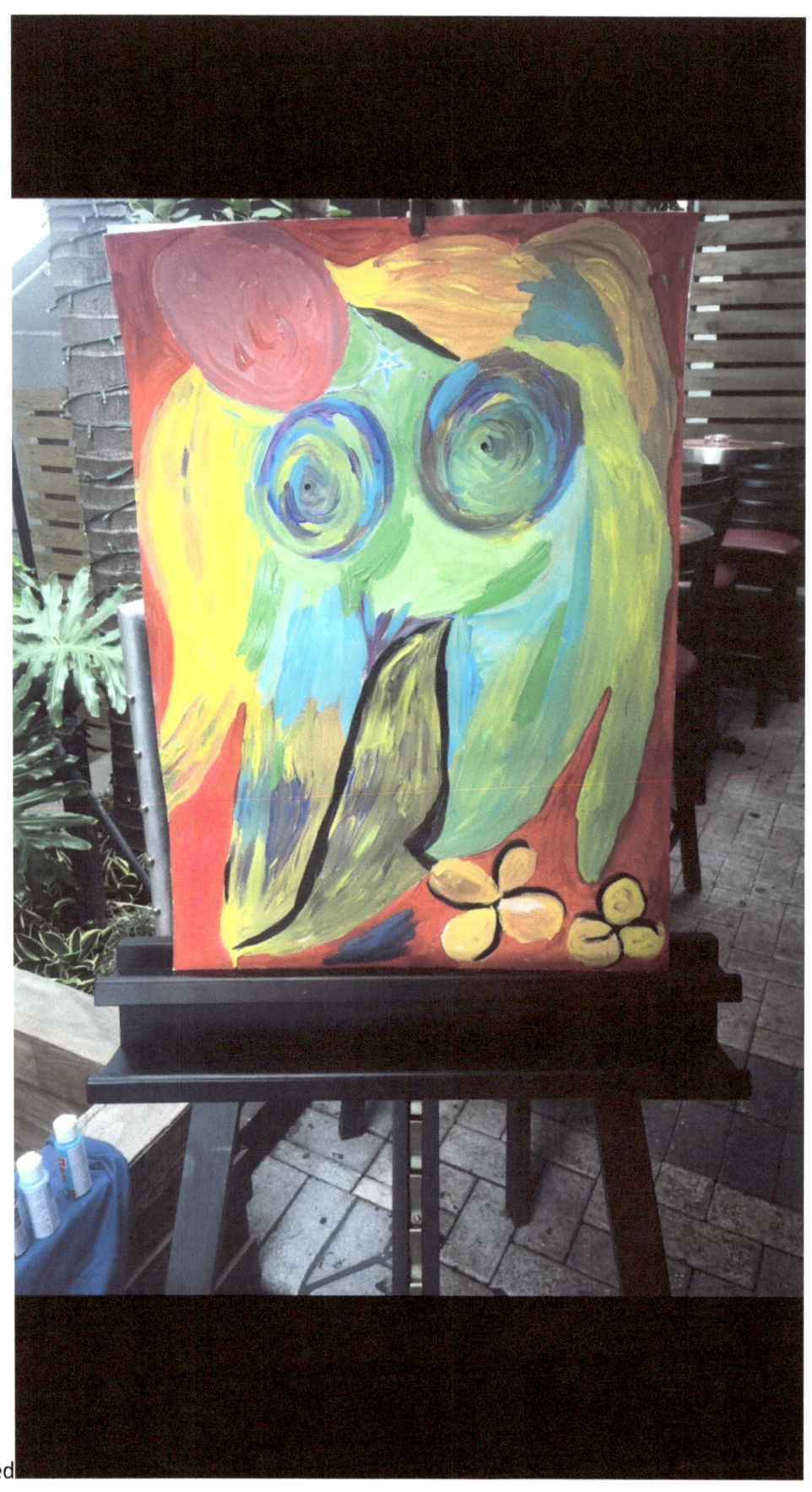

Untitled

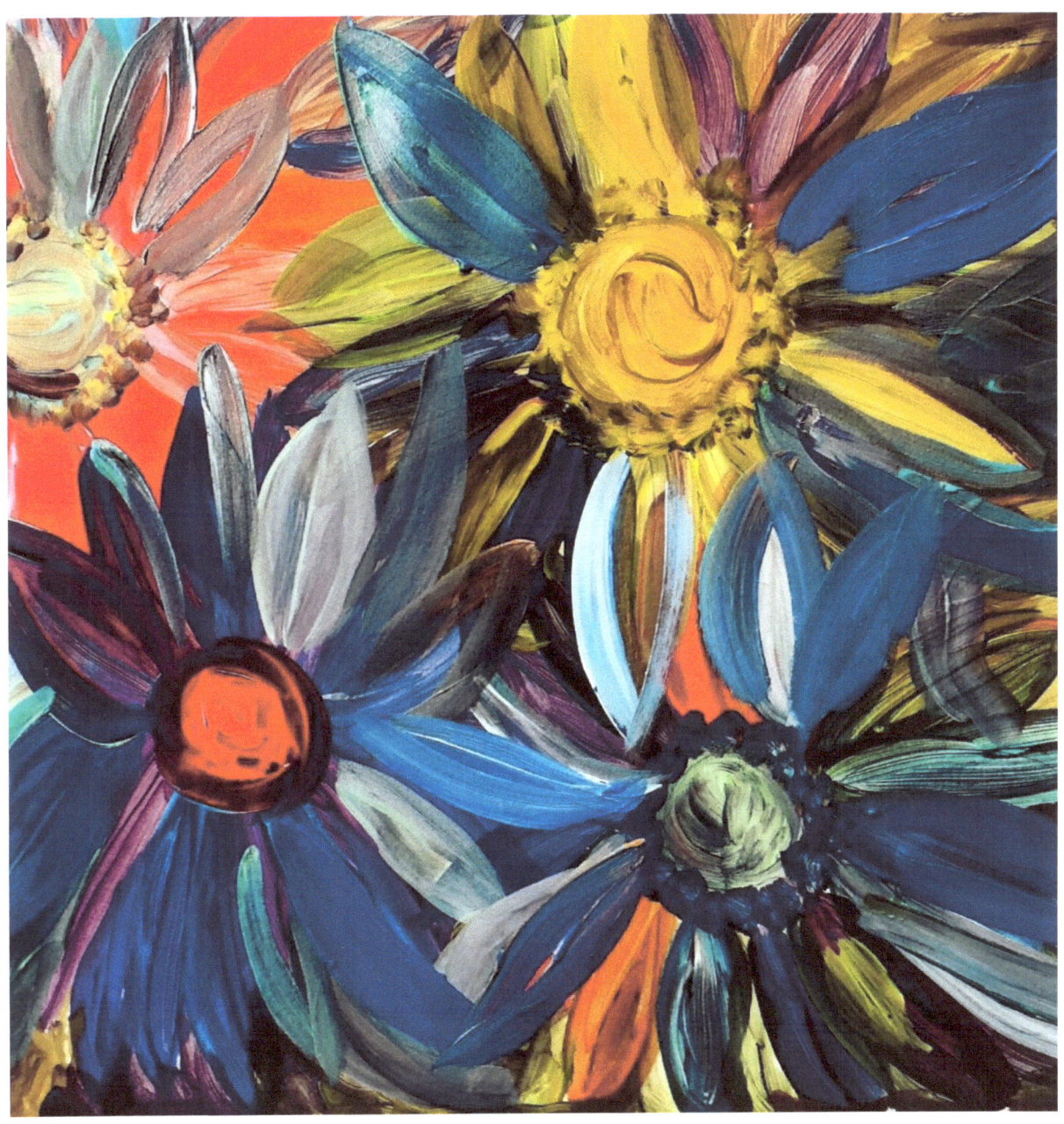

FLORAL FOR SHIRTS AND SCARVES

I like to design for clothing. I have offered my art for reproduction on t-shirts, scarves and hats

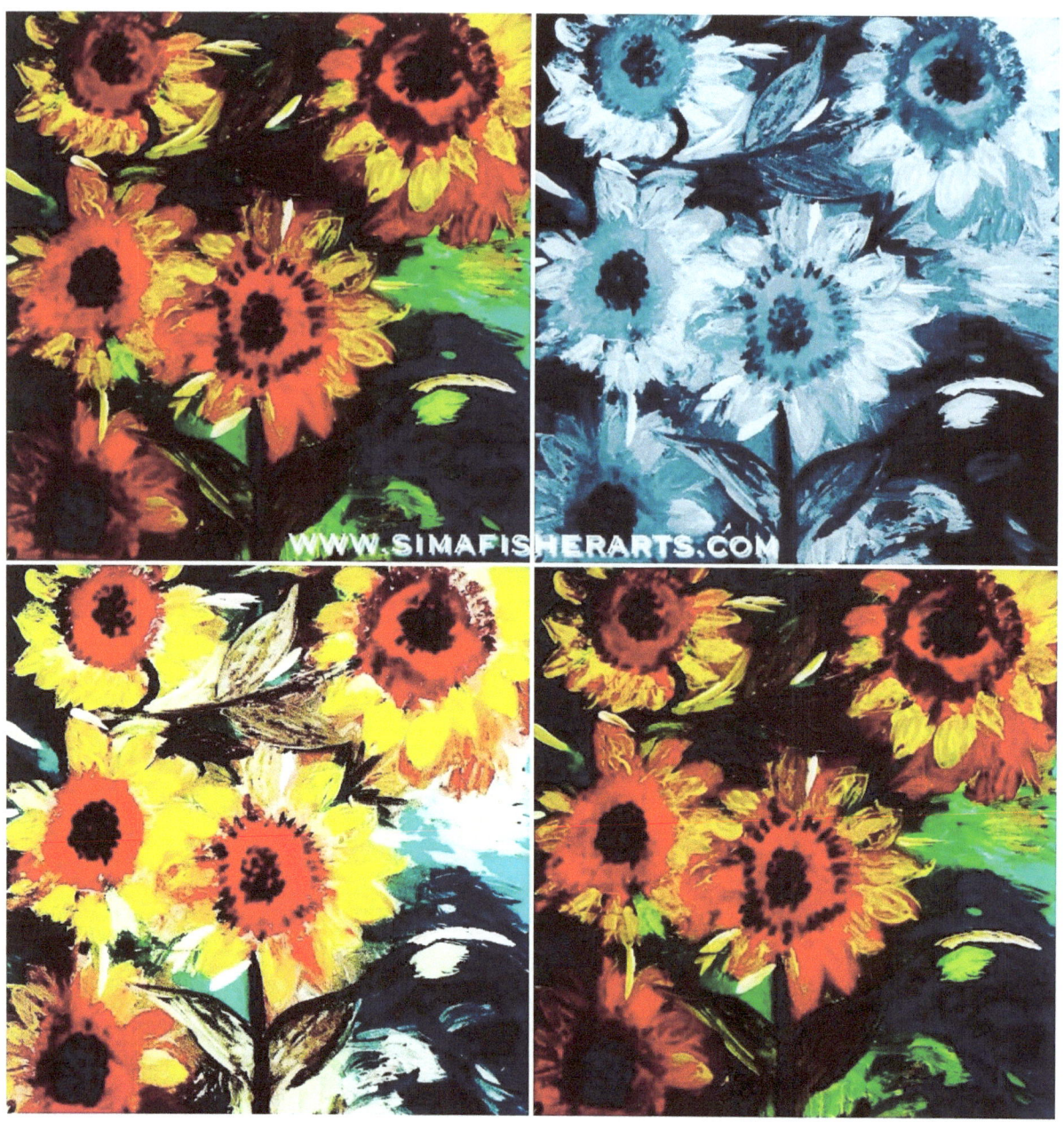

SUNFLOWERS. I love to adjust the colors of my paintings. Same painting with different colors and give it a different feel and temperature.

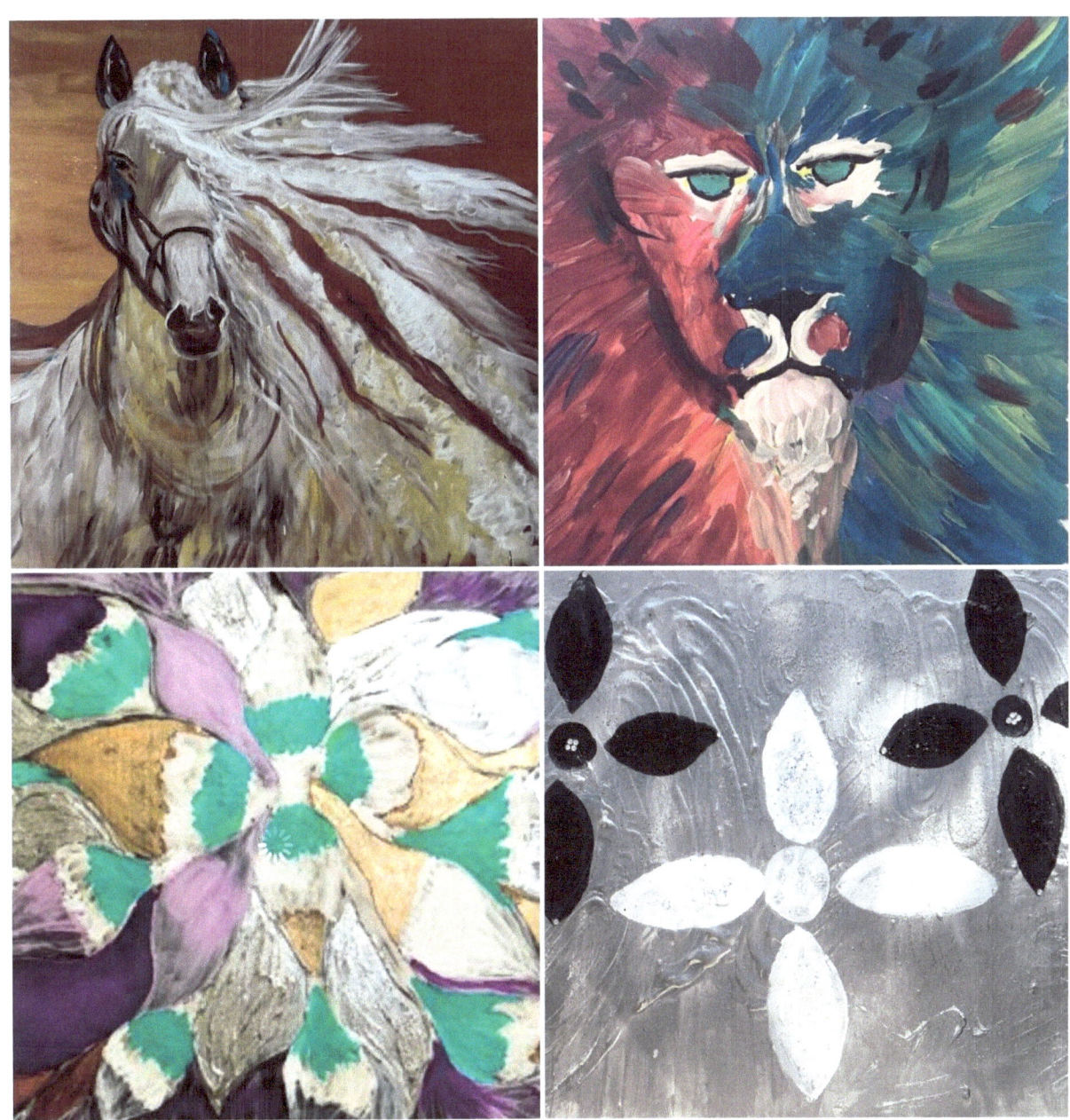

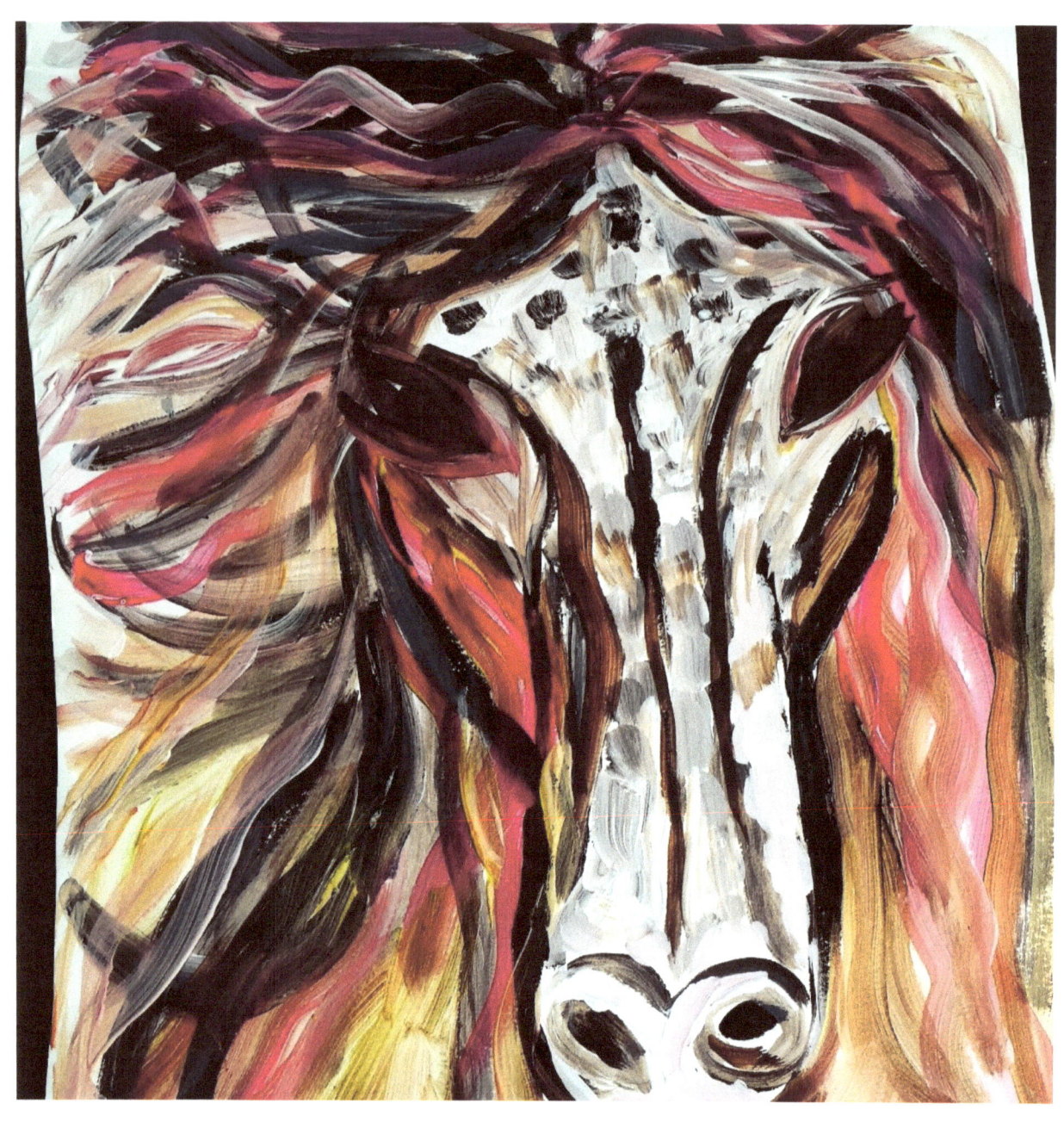

ANGRY RED HORSE

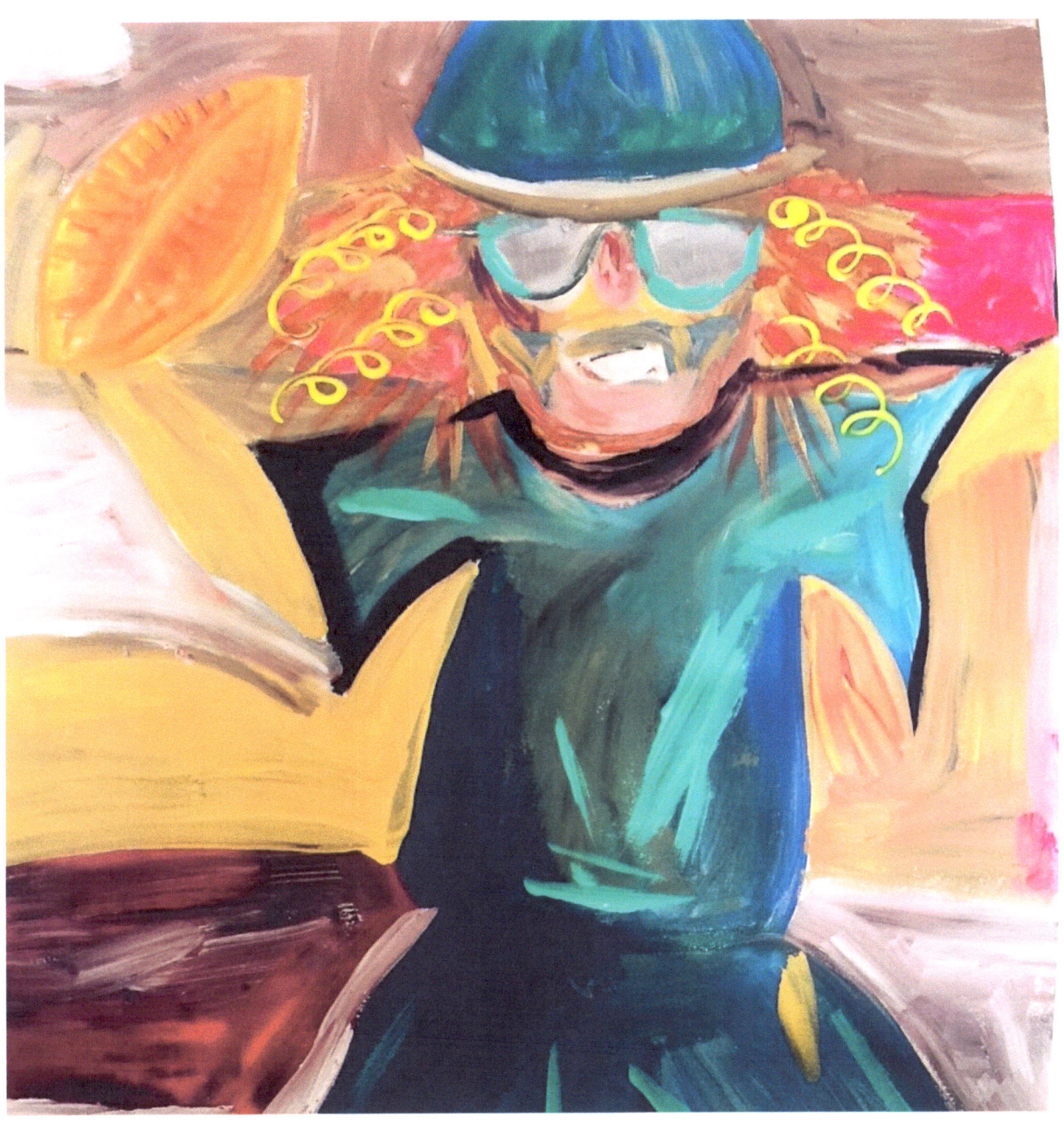

ABSTRACT MORACCO

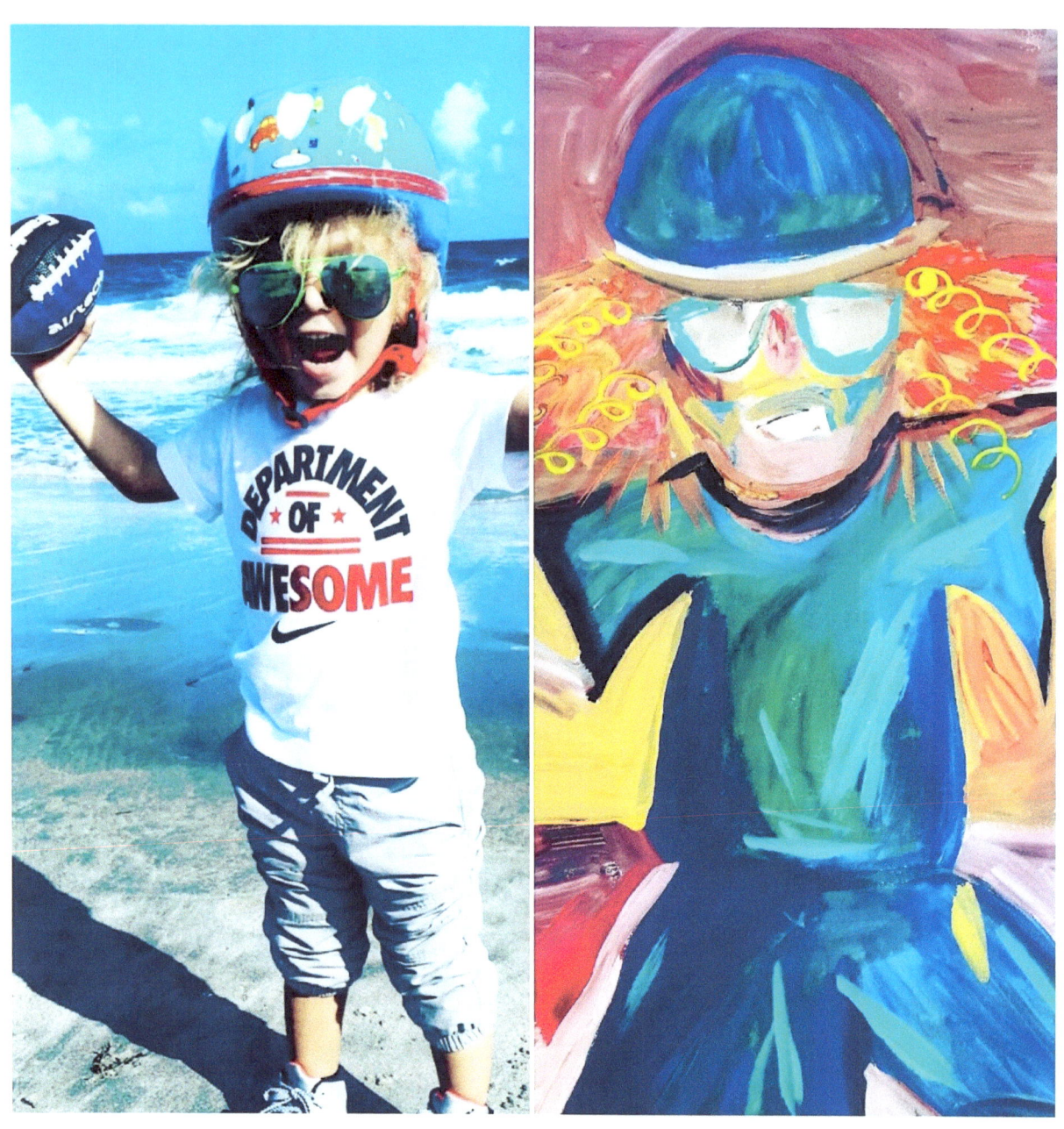

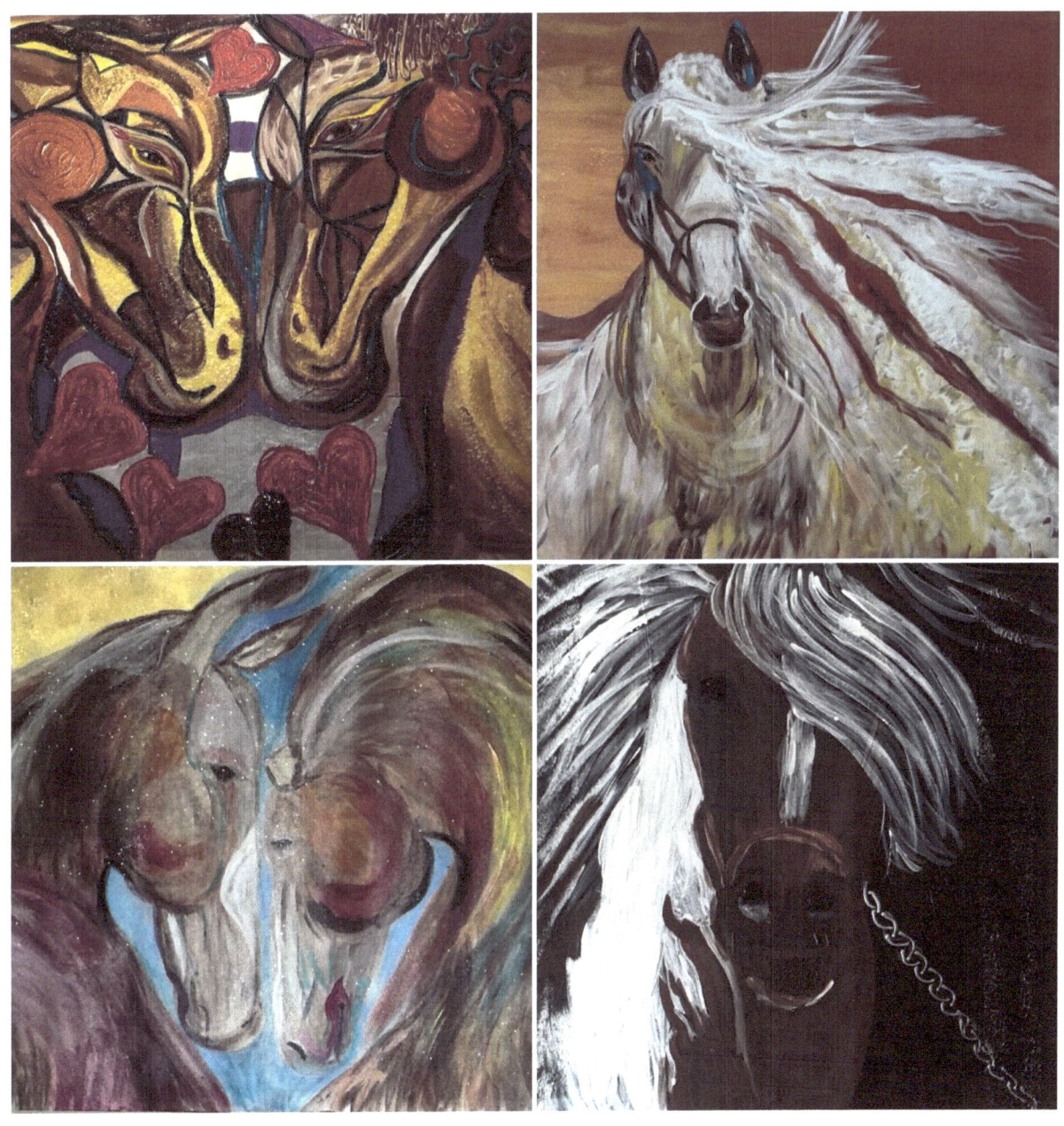

HORSES SERIES

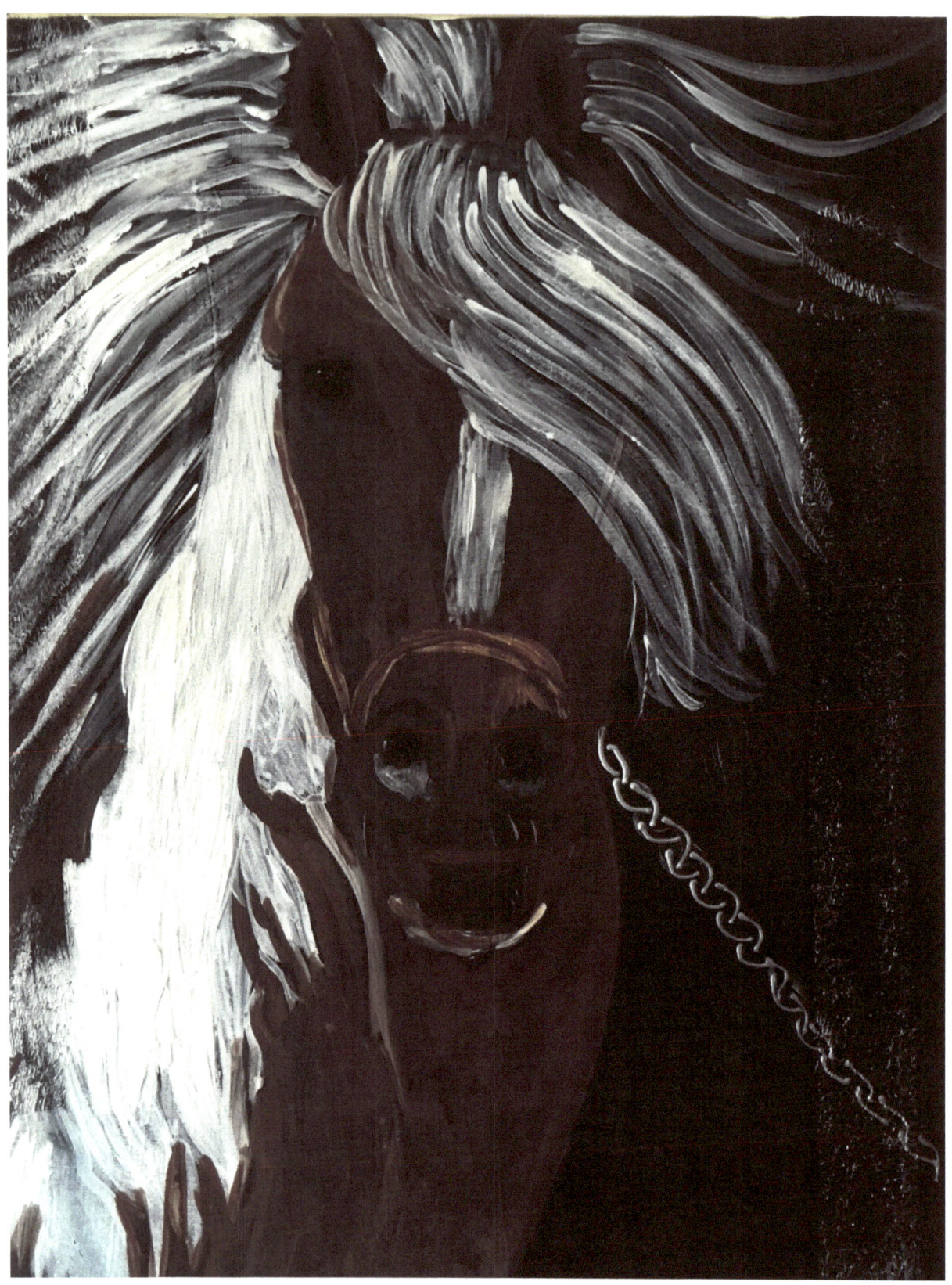

DARK HORSE-Commissioned piece

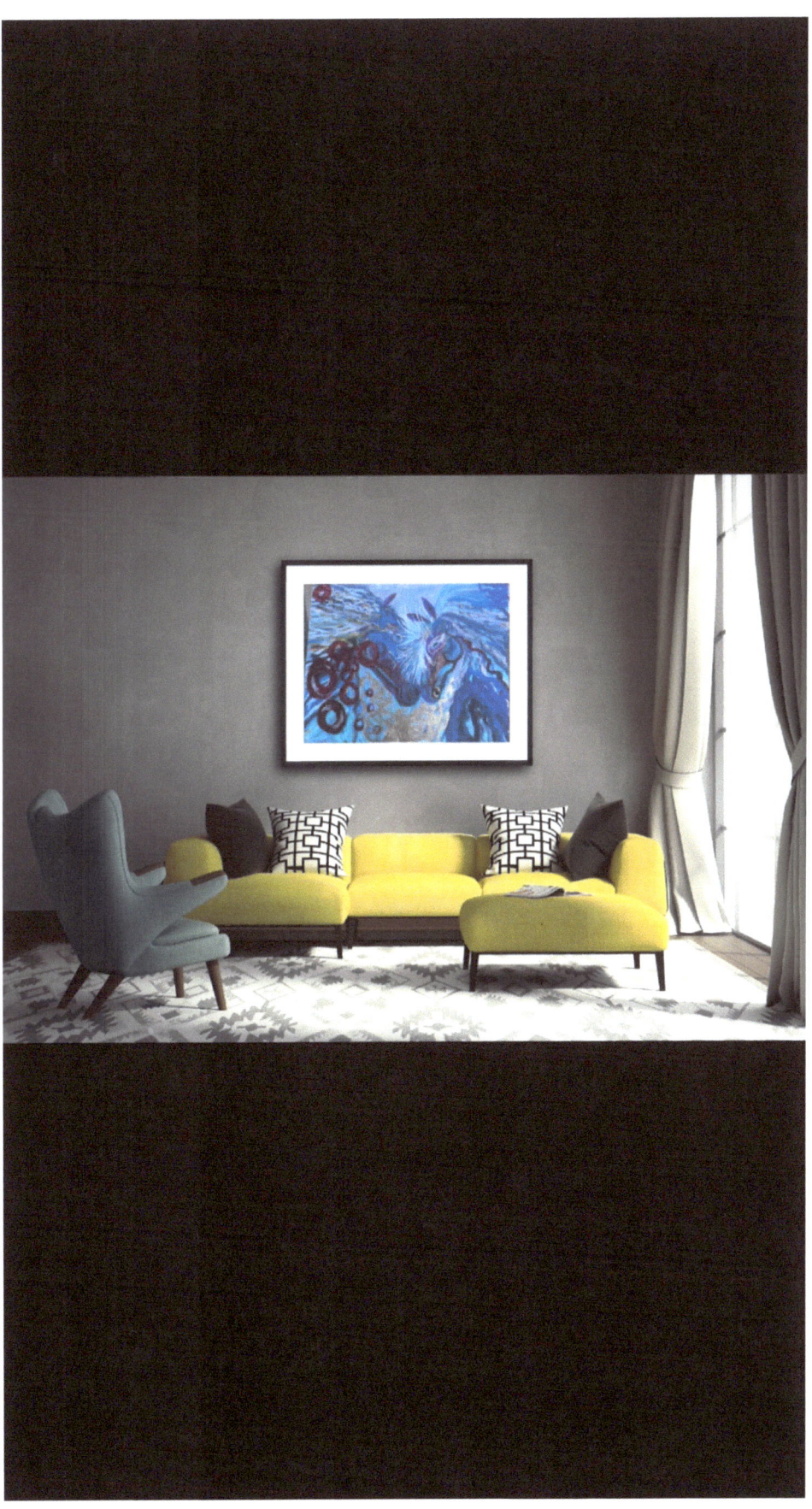

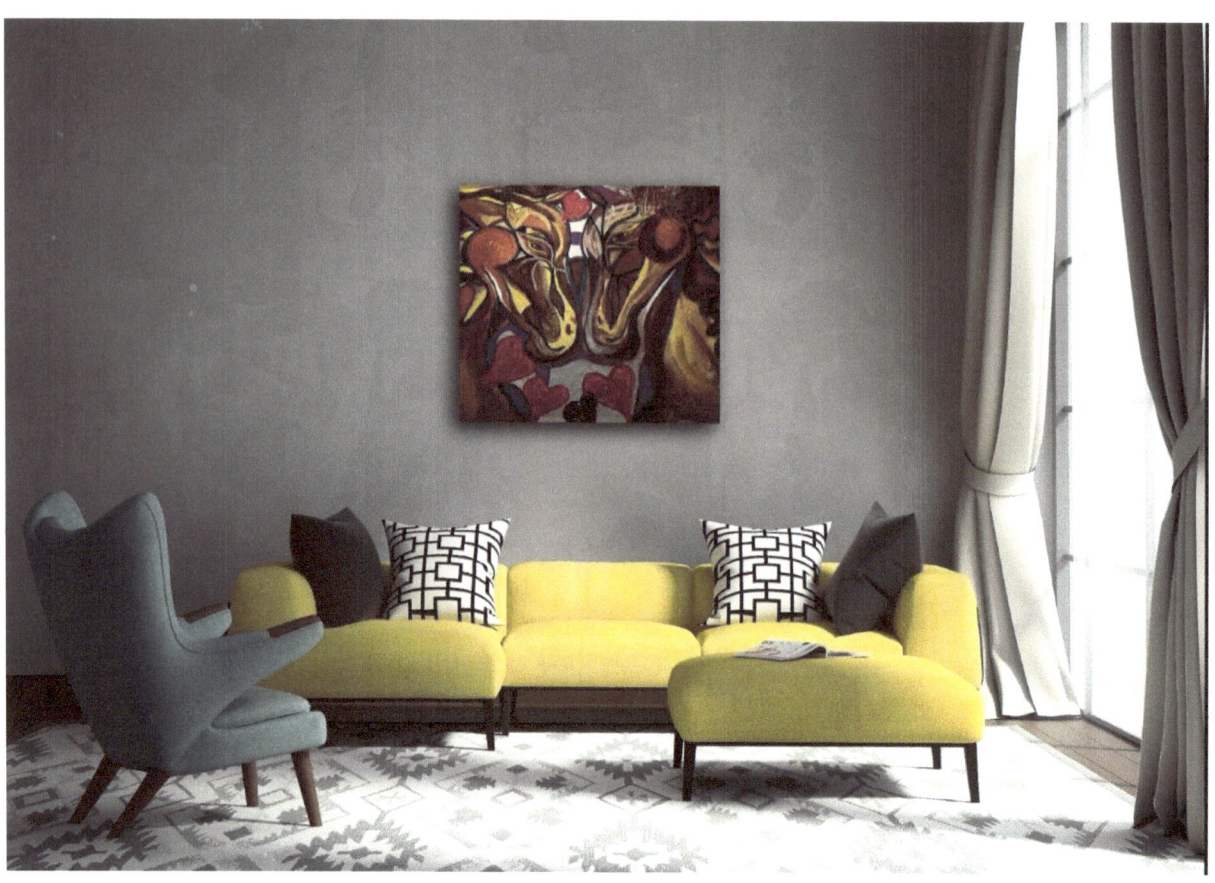

Vibrant colors that match furniture and home décor. We offer our beautiful styles to interior designers and home decorators.

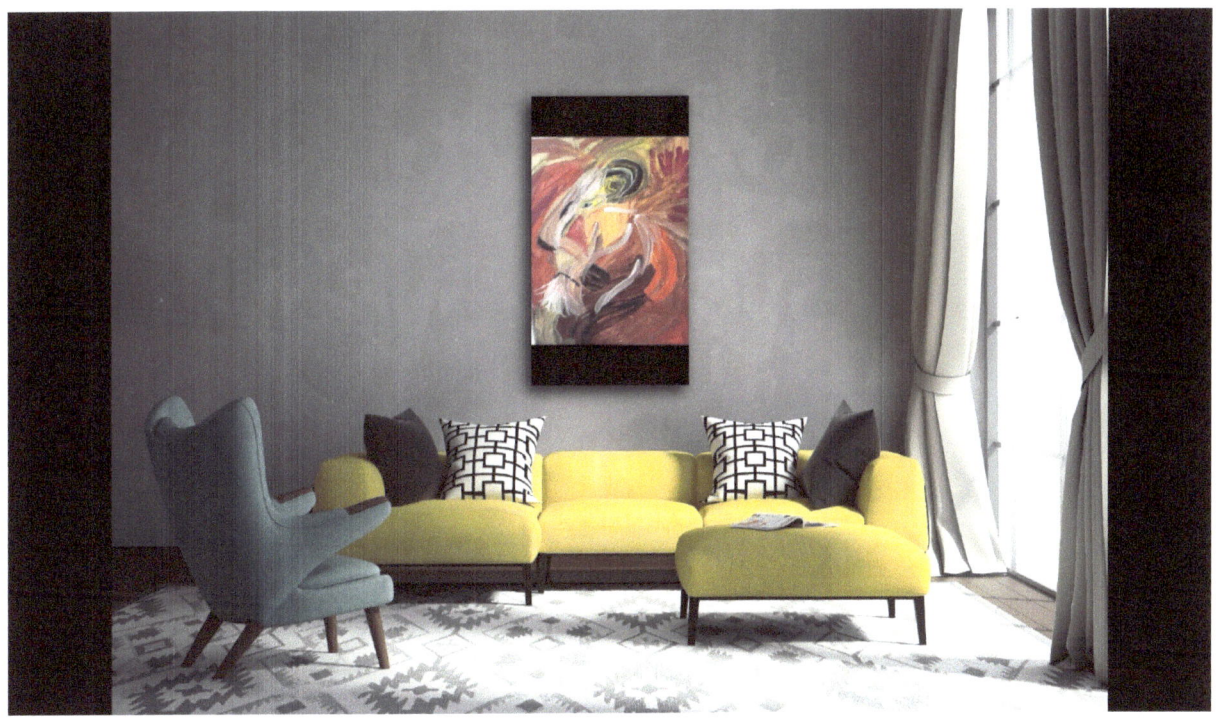

Home Décor Paintings

Many home décor specialist come to me and ask me to paint for them. I offer a wide variety of styles and colors for home decorations. Vibrant colors, all sizes.

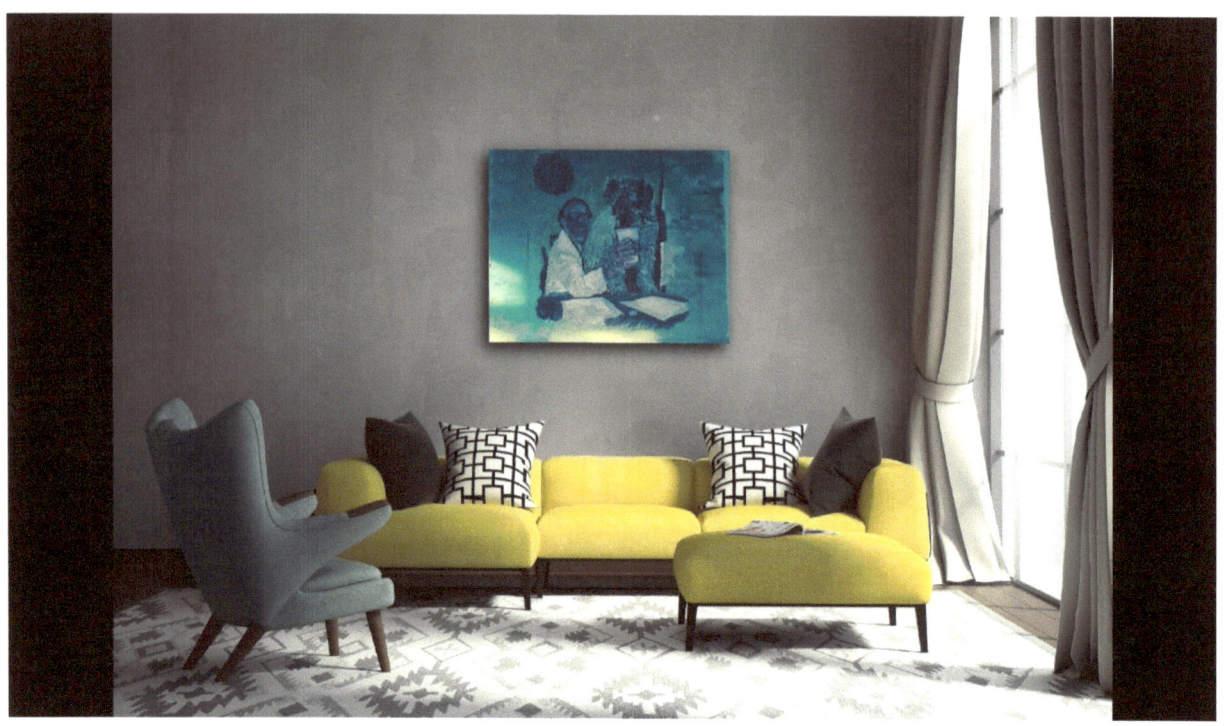

I have painted many portraits for clients and their animals. I love taking on projects that challenge me to be creative and make my clients happy. It is a spiritual gift I like to give.

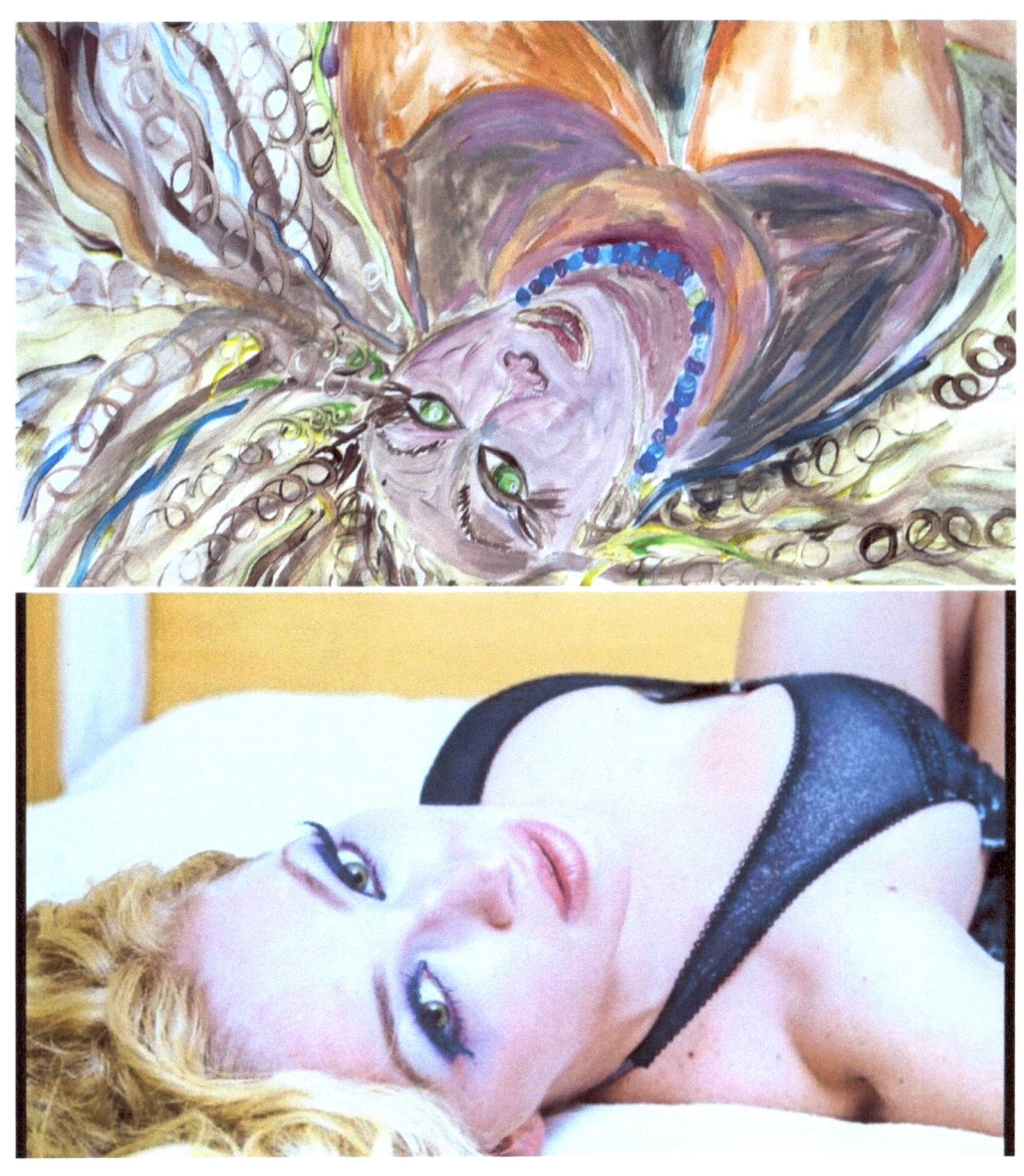

SELF PORTRAIT of Sima Fisher. Abstract.

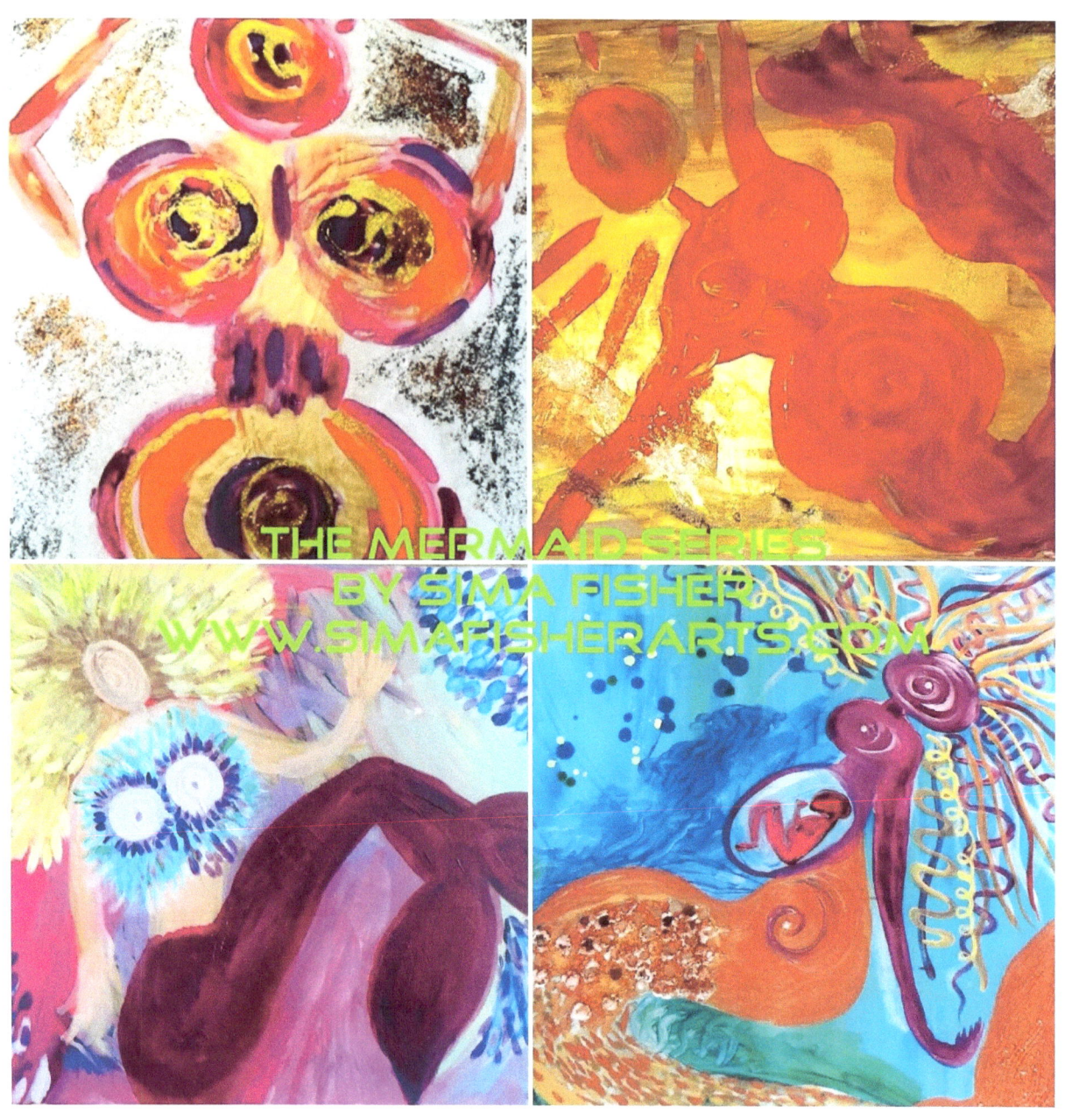

Mermaid Series

Sima Fisher has painted many "series" of paintings including the Mermaid Series

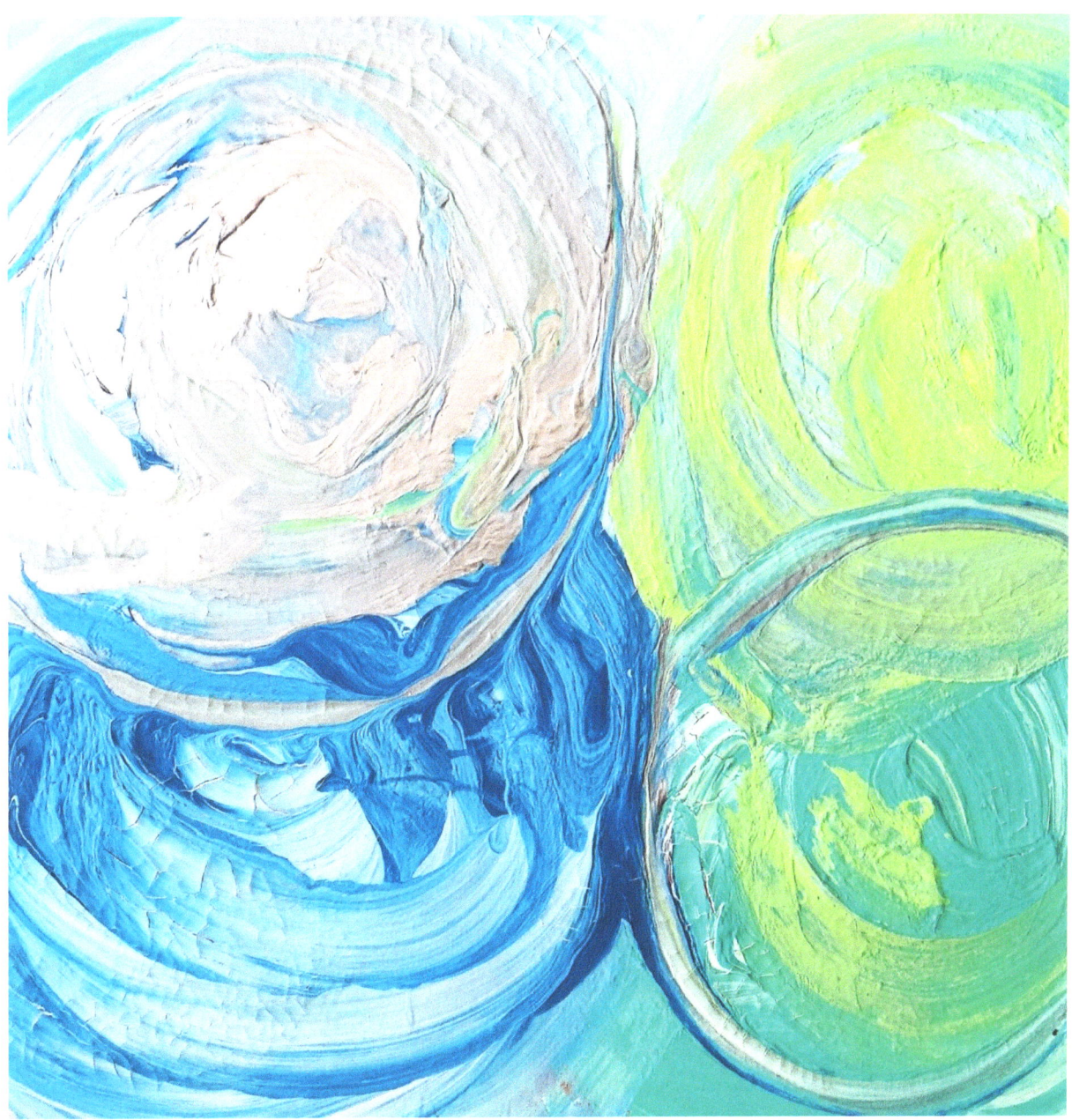

Home Décor Ideas and Sketches that help to inspire the eye

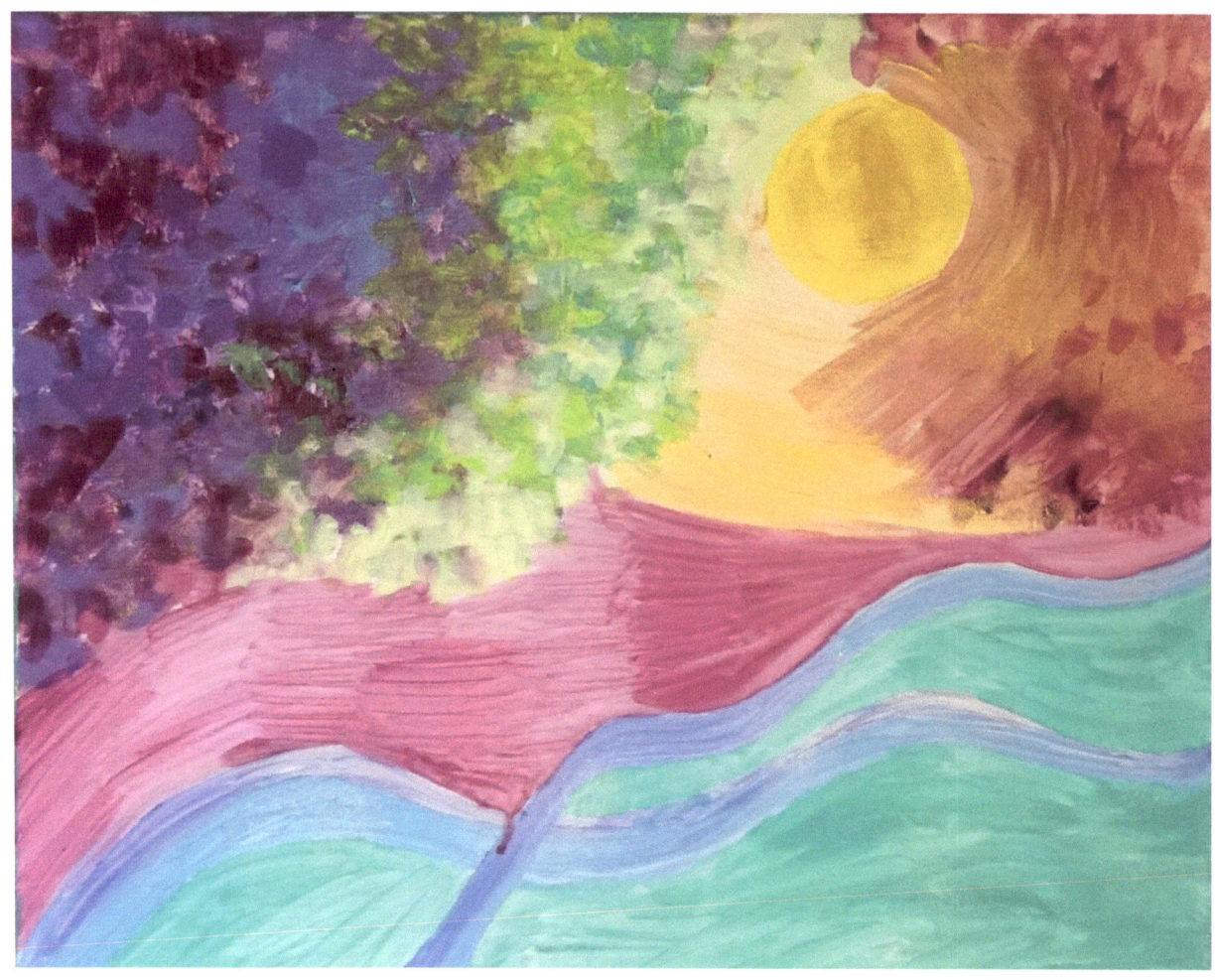

Paintings are usually layered but this one I decided to keep it very simple.

Songwriting by Sima Fisher

My First Album I ever wrote was with my best friend Alex Franco from Mississauga Ontario Canada. We used to sit in his studio coming up with ideas for songs and experimenting with the art of it.

Set Me Free Album

Set Me Free

I wanna feel the sand in between my toes

Only the ocean knows how good it feels

I wanna swim out far so no one can see me but the fish

They bite my toes

I love it

It tickles

Set me free now Set me free

Let me be now

Set me free now set me free

Let me be now let me be.

Give A Little Love

Give a little love tonight

Give a little love all right

Oooo oooh oooh ooh oh oh oh

Stars

Stars Hey, Hey

We see the Stars

Everyone round here keeps coming around

They all wanna see the new girl in town

They're all jealous cause we see the star

And we see the Stars

Hey Hey You know I know you know

We see the stars

Love and Solutions

Everybody has a different kind of love

It all depends on how we're taught to love

But you know the kind I want

Could take me years to find

Oh oh I ache all over

Love and Solutions

Is what we want now?

Love and Solutions

Is what we got now?

Love and solutions

For the record

Love and solutions

Makes me better

Waiting for You

I'm waiting for you

I'm waiting for you

I'm waiting for you

Naked After Dark

You're so worried about doing things right

You're so worried about who may see us fight

Let's get together baby

Meet me in the park

Let's get together baby

Naked after dark

Being Alone

I'm not good at being alone

I'm not good at staying home

I like the crazy things in life

I love staying up all night

I'm sorry I can't stay true to you

I'm sorry I can't stay true

Little Girl

Hey Hey little girl

Coming down the hall

Taking away my man

Who was once my all

Hey Hey little girl

You mean nothing to me

He's not the only one to be please

Oh can't you see

His heart belongs to me

He'll come running back you'll see

Without You-by Sima Fisher and Alex Franco (Neon Music)

I'm tired of feeling so blue

I don't want to be number two

Why is it that everyone wants you?

The nights are so lonely without you

I'm spinning around in my head

I never told you this before

I need you forever more

Lonely lonely without you

The second album that I wrote was with Peter Prislesnik in his studio in downtown Toronto. We took the very talented Simon Wilcox in as a songwriter and finished it off with Producer Shawn. Eddie Bullen (producer of "Hands Up" The Club Med song) to make the song Make U Sweat.

City Lights Album

City Lights

The people in the streets

They just push and shove

The people in the clubs they just grind for love

The people push and grab

I'm so tired of waiting for the subway cars

I'm so tired of waiting for these street cars

And then my car gets toes

I just feel so old

I feel unsanitary is this all necessary?

Is it all necessary?

But when I get home to you

I see I see only you

And when one becomes two I see I see only you

What you mean to me

You're all I live for

What I mean to you, you're all I live for too

I remember

I remember when we met

Days like those I can't forget

Things I did and didn't do

Disappear when I'm with you

I'll give it

You need it

Are you ready to receive it?

I'll give it

You need it

I wanna give you all you ever needed

Hold' ON

Dreams

Ten Years

Small

When we were small

We didn't really care at all

If anything was perfect yah

We moved from one thing till the next and we were

So happy just to play all day

We used to laugh

Used to cry

Used to play all day till the street lights came on and she'd say

She'd say

Don't forget about the past

The things we've known forever

The things we used to love

We get old so fast

We thought that we were clever

Never say never

No no

No no no

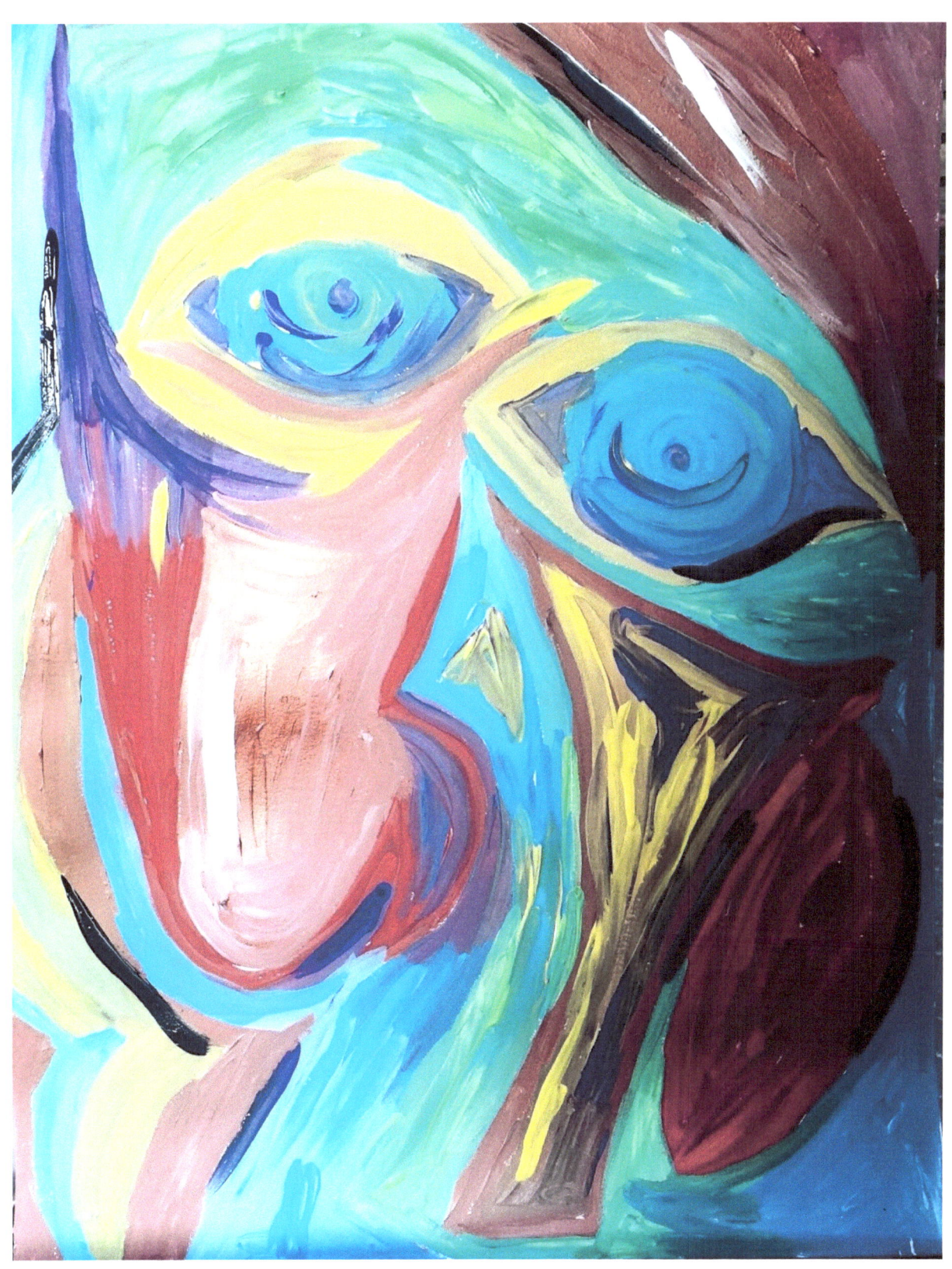

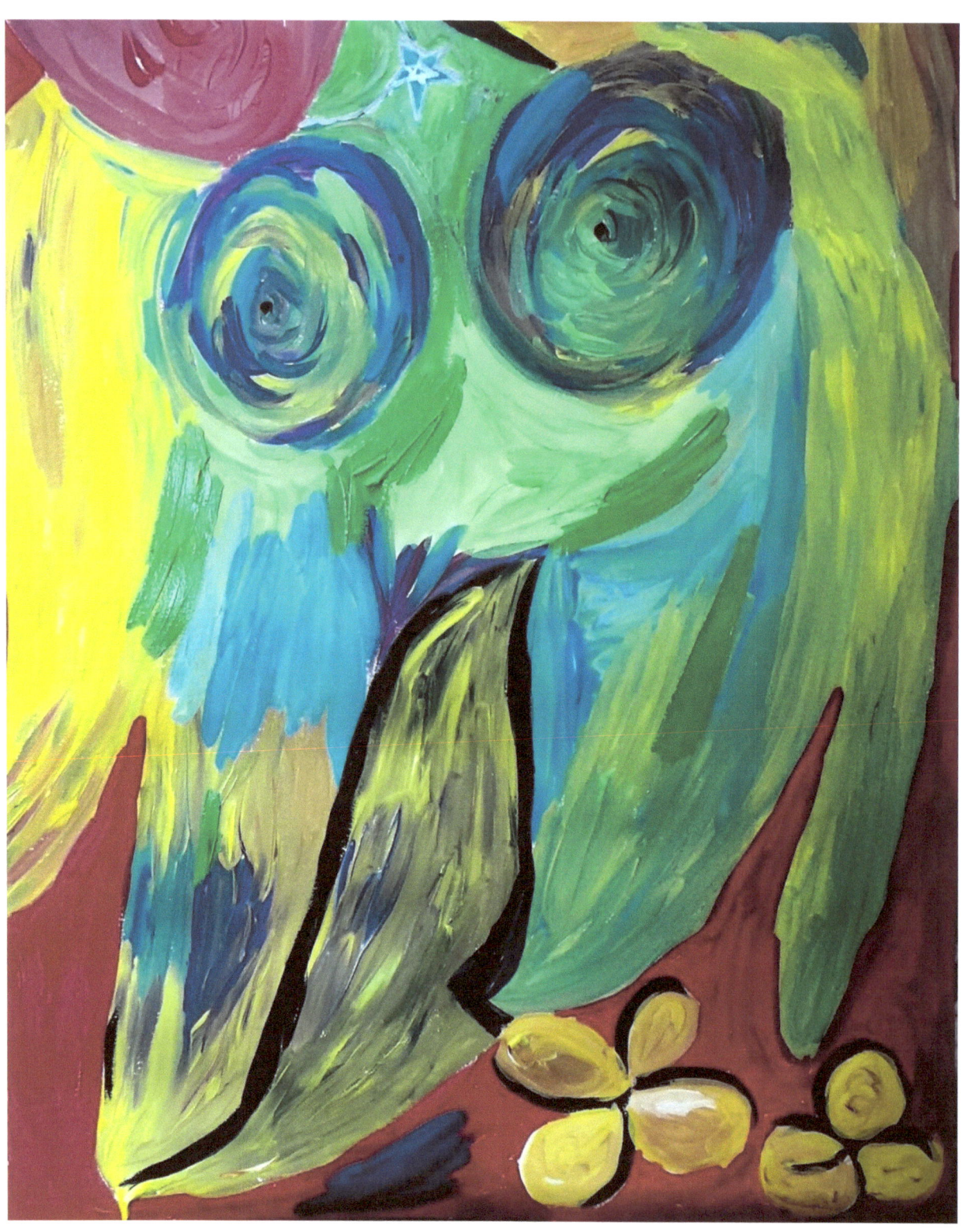

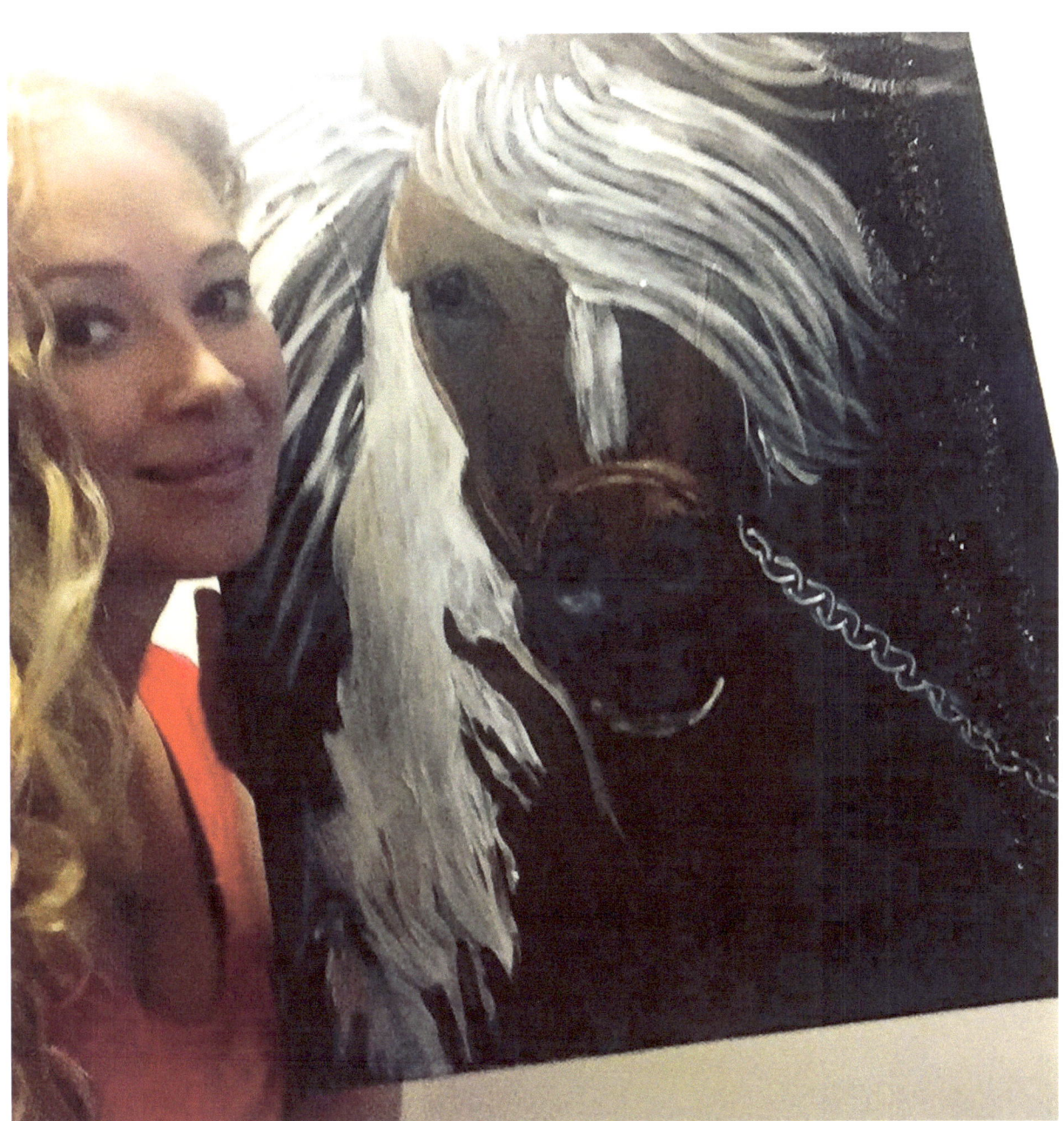

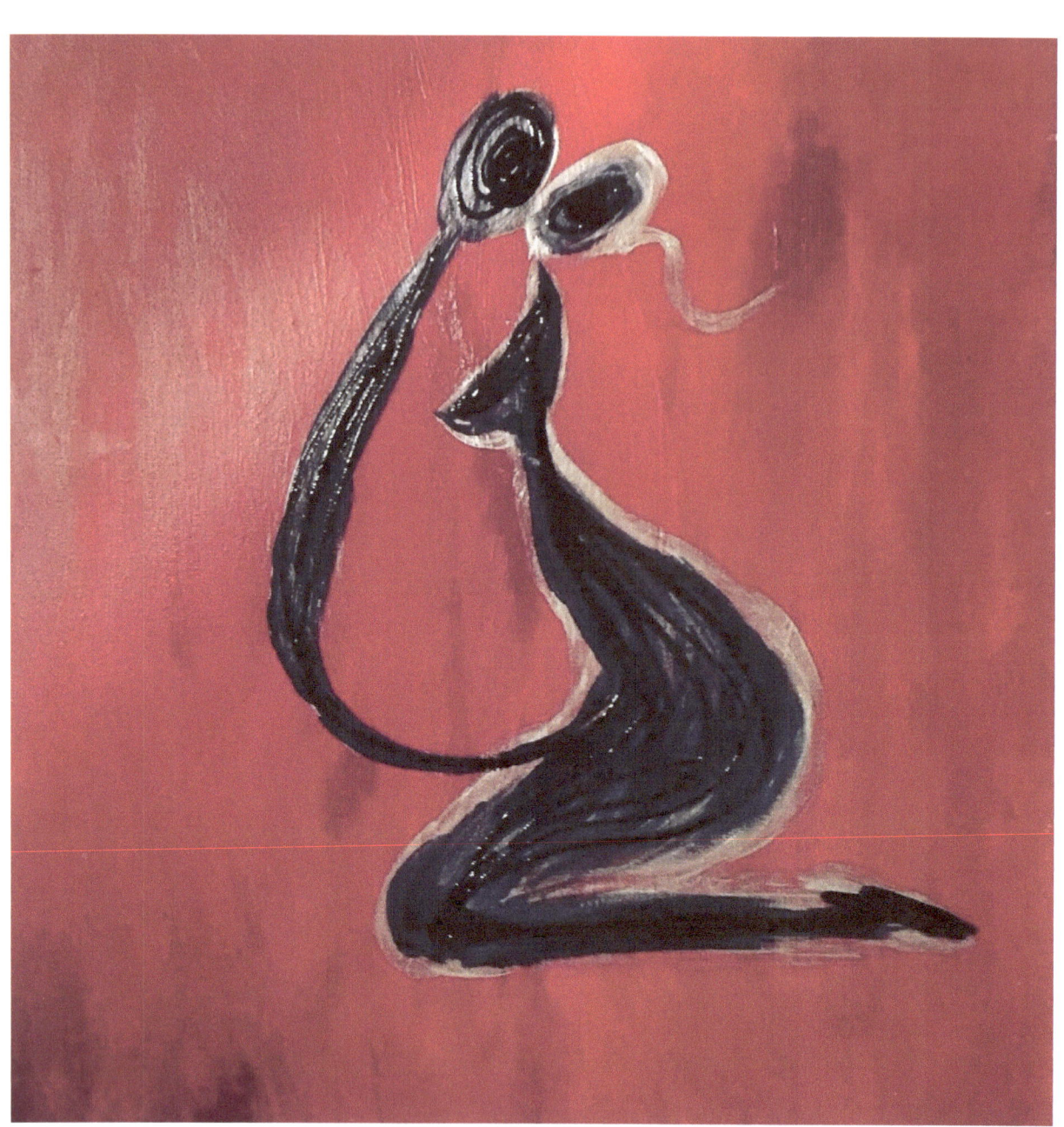

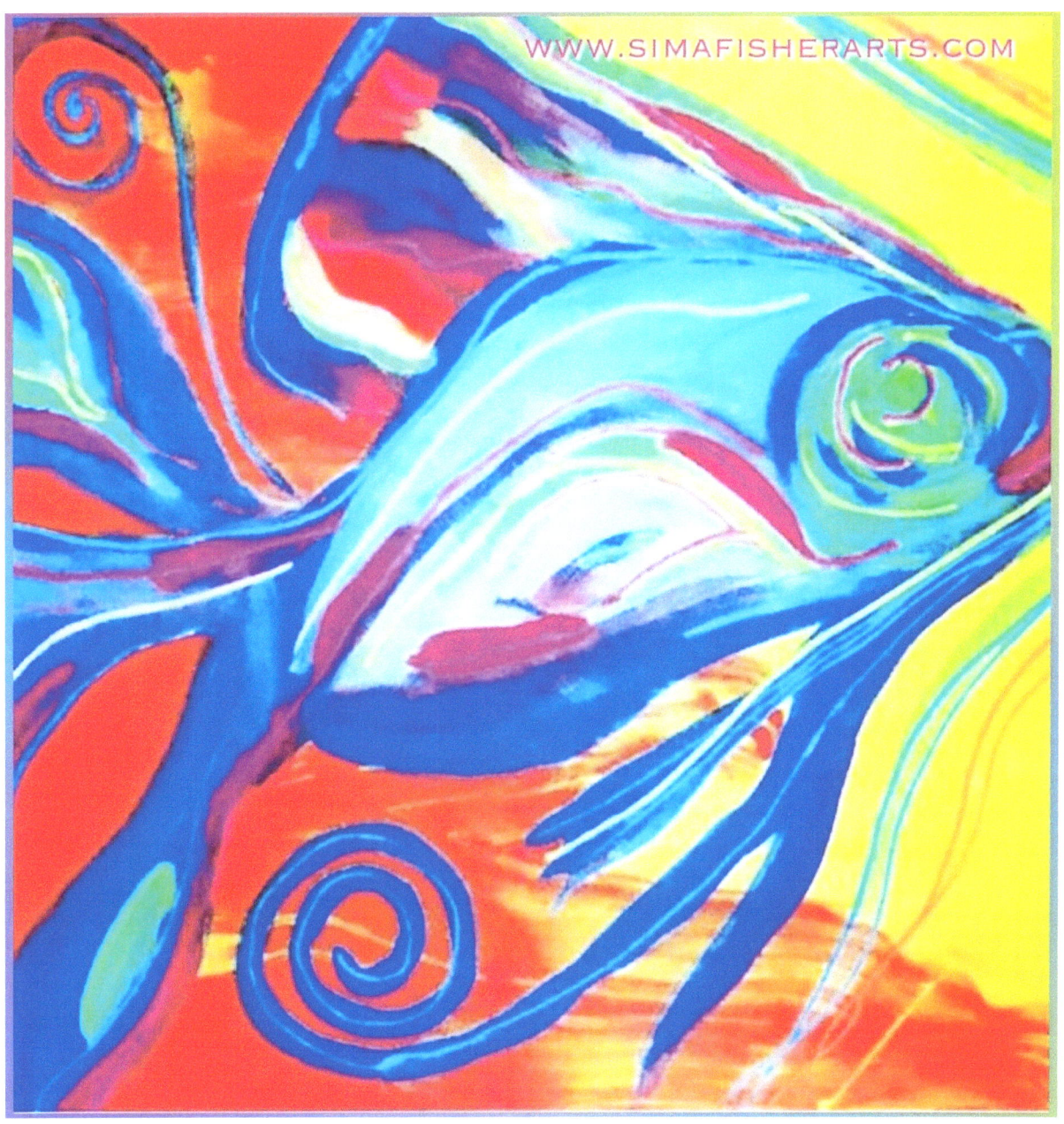

FISH FOR HEALING

I create this vibrantly colored fish for a rehab Center. They loved the colors

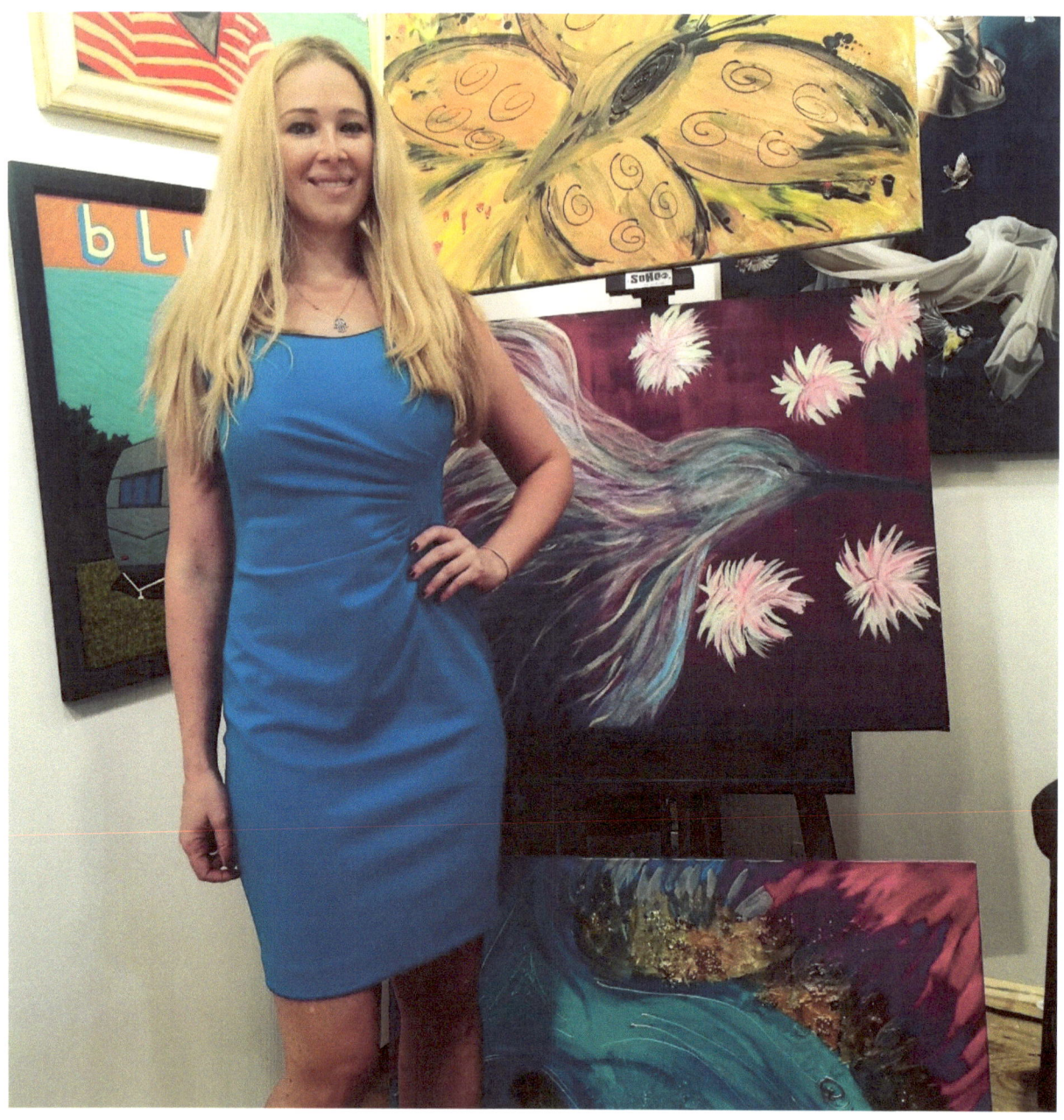

I showcase my work at festivals and my work was feature in the International Magazine. THE RED DOT ART FAIR during Miami Art Basel was one of the events I attended. I was interviewed by HEART TO ART and Featured in Art Tour International Magazine. (SEE NEXT PAGE FOR ARTICLE)

SIMA FISHER

Explorations Of Nature
by Viviana Puello

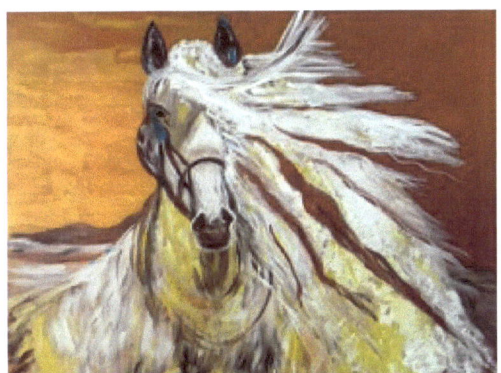

"Horses in Love" Mixed Media On Canvas

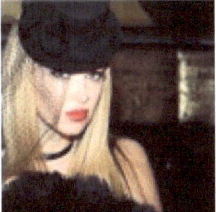

Multi-award artist Sima Fisher has captured the interest of the international art scene with her Expressionistic, colorist interpretations of art.

Fisher towards her love for nature, animals, and we can encounter them with all loving beings in her work. Through layers of color, watercolor, and acrylic, Fisher explores the connection of painting nature and spectacular. By creating contemplative works of art that respect the relationship between a vision and the universe. Her images serve to portray the graphic textured space fashioned from a more wide nature.

Sima Fisher is inspired by Fisher's has qualified her to explore multiple creative avenues, such as poetry, songwriting, acting, and painting. Her...

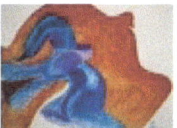

"Love Birds" Mixed Media On Canvas

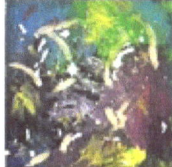

"Sunny Flowers" Mixed Media On Canvas

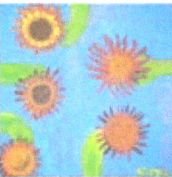

"Sunny Flowers" Mixed Media On Canvas

www.simafisherarts.com

"Horses in Love" Mixed Media On Canvas

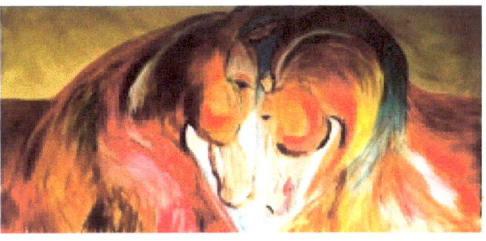

ART TOUR INTERNATIONAL MAGAZINE FEATURED.-Interviewed by VIVIANA PUELLO

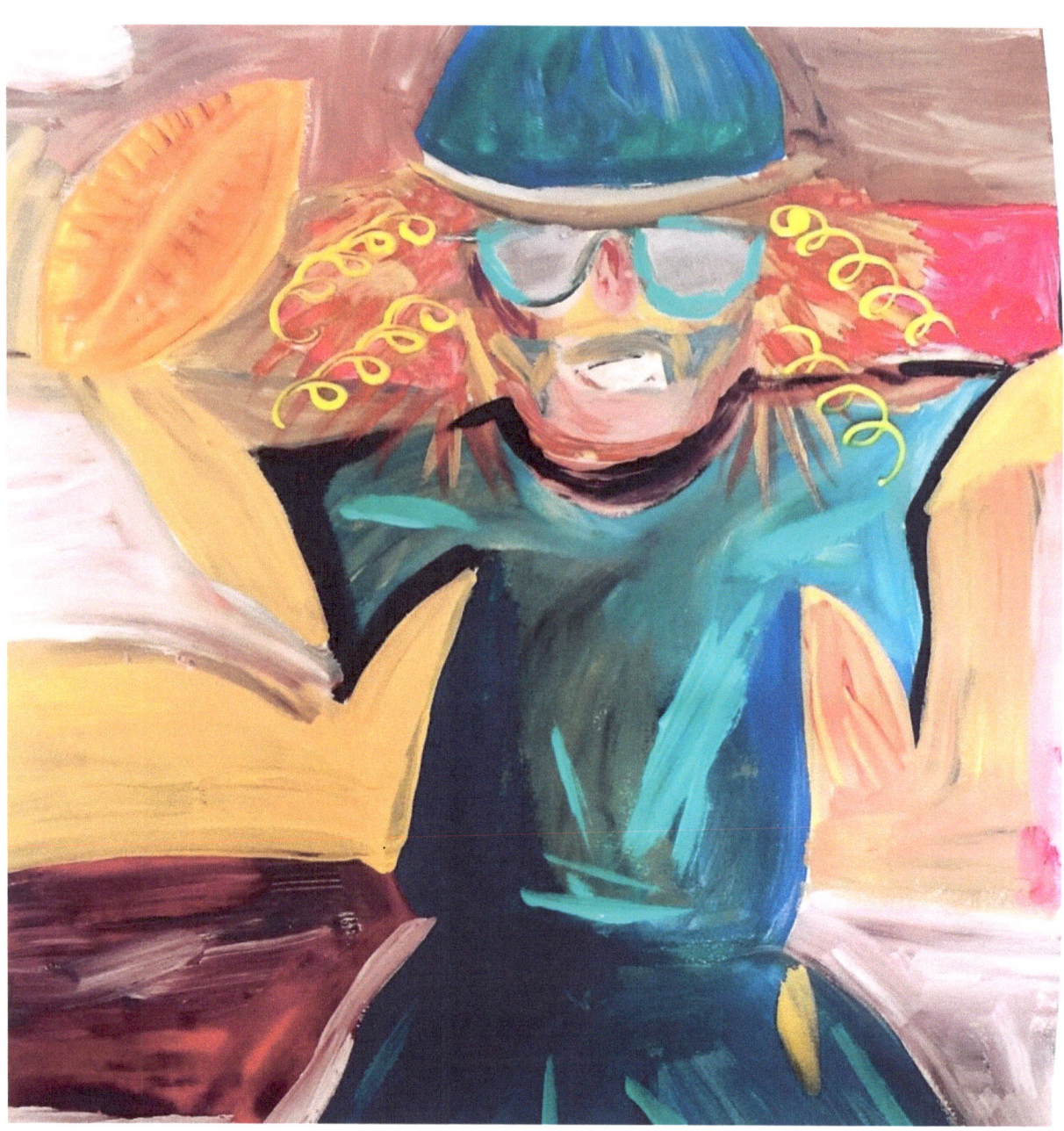

MORACCO CHACHO the BALLER!

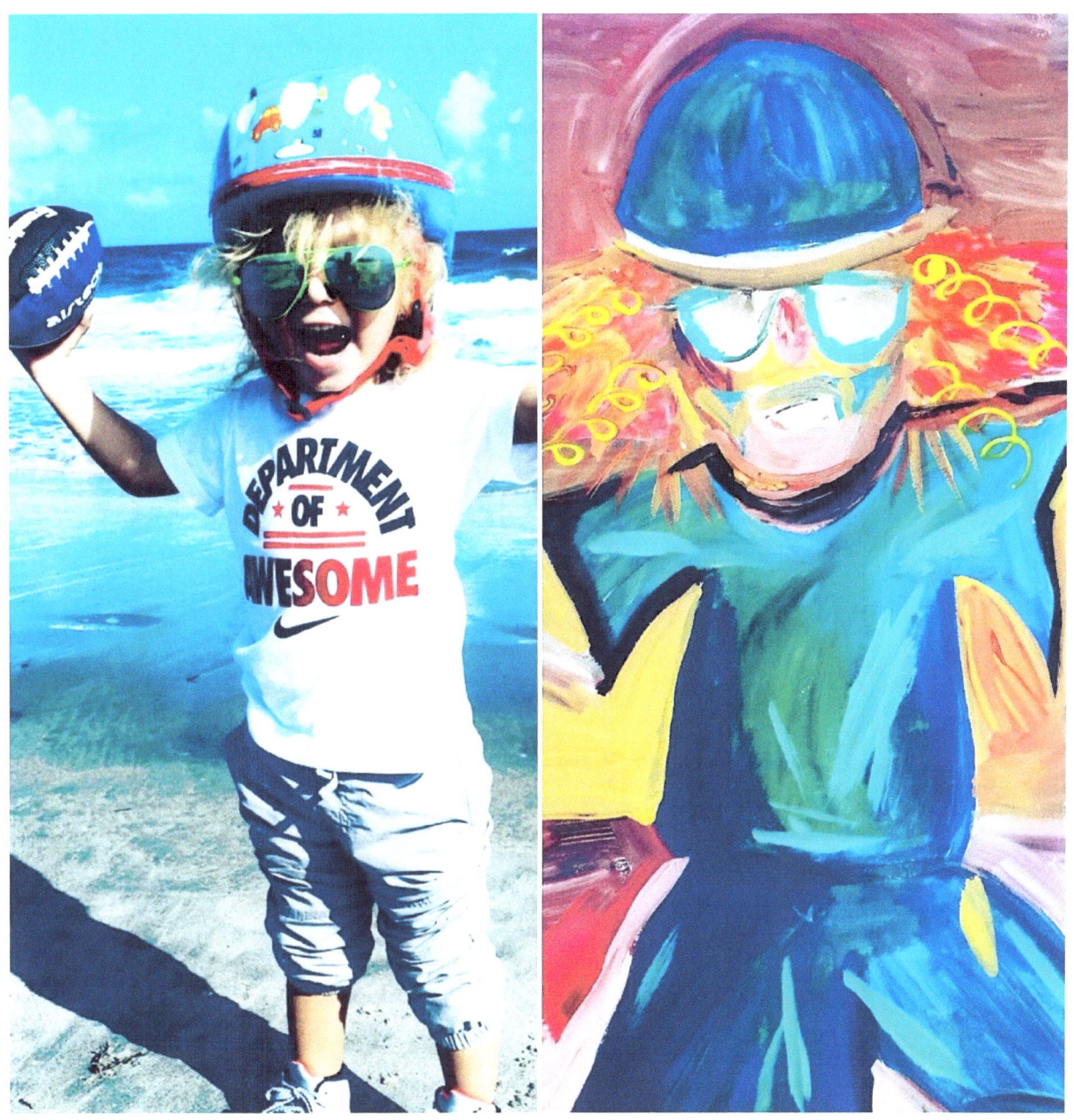

One of my favorite subjects is painting my Son Moracco. He is a true athlete!

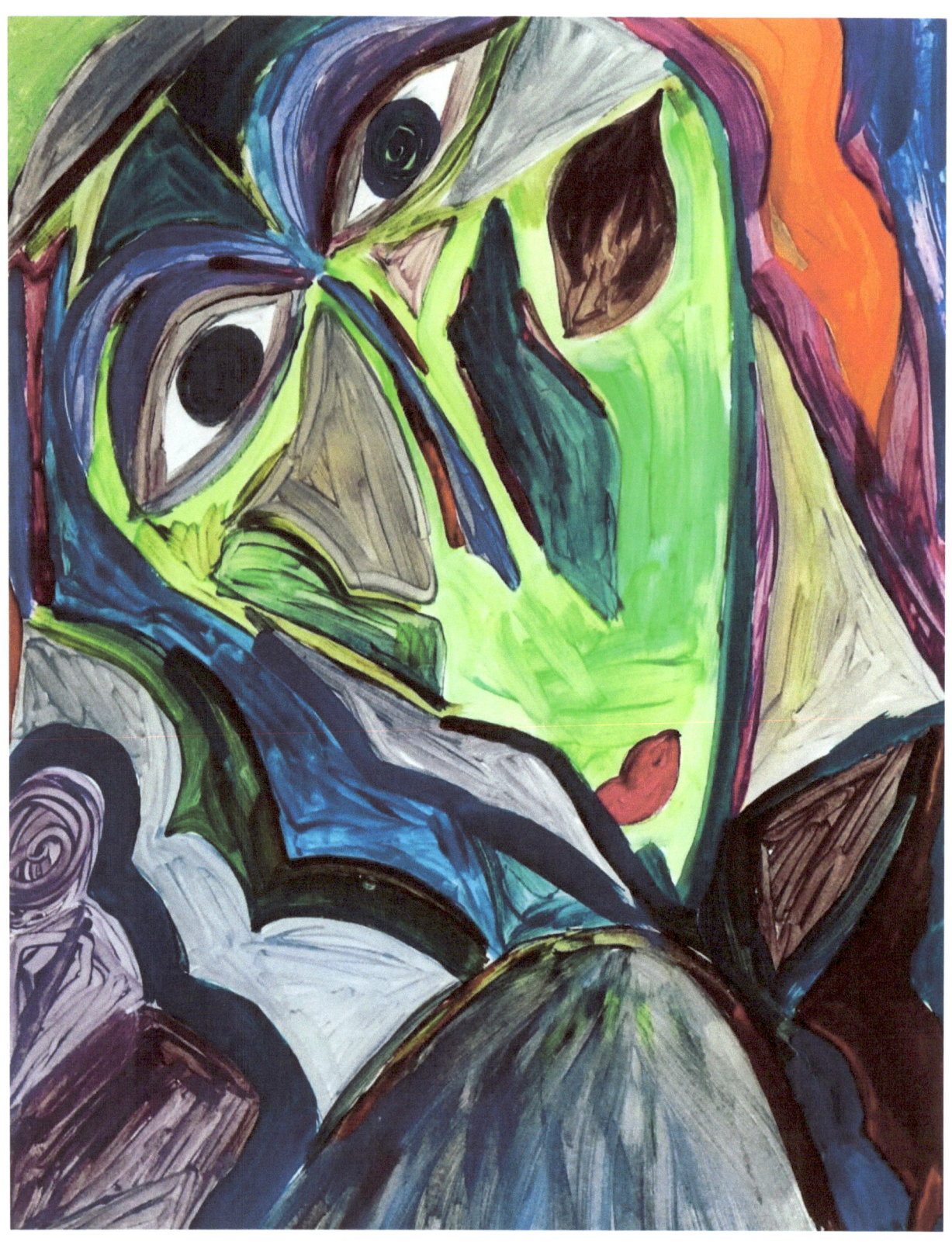

SURPRISED LADY

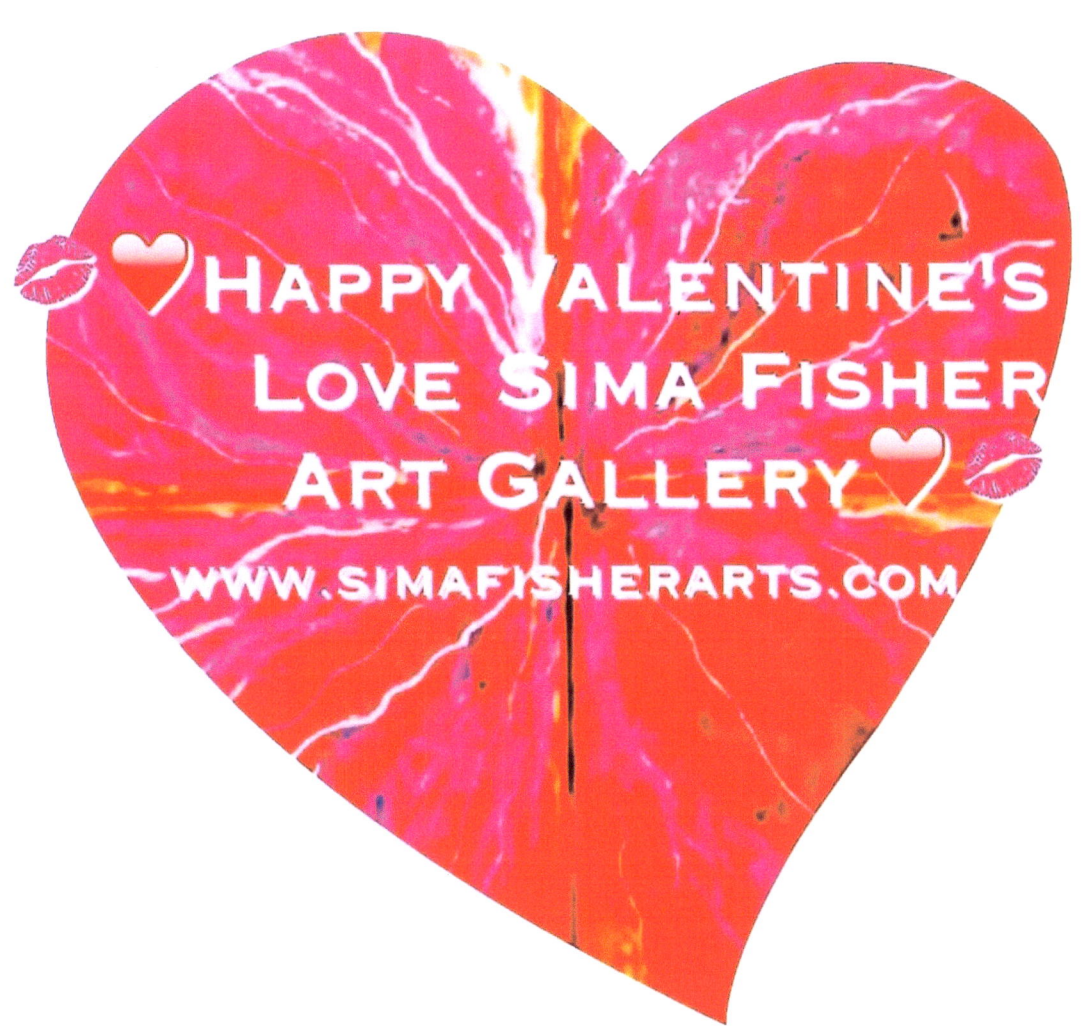

HAPPY VALENTINE'S
LOVE SIMA FISHER
ART GALLERY
WWW.SIMAFISHERARTS.COM

SWEET LOVE

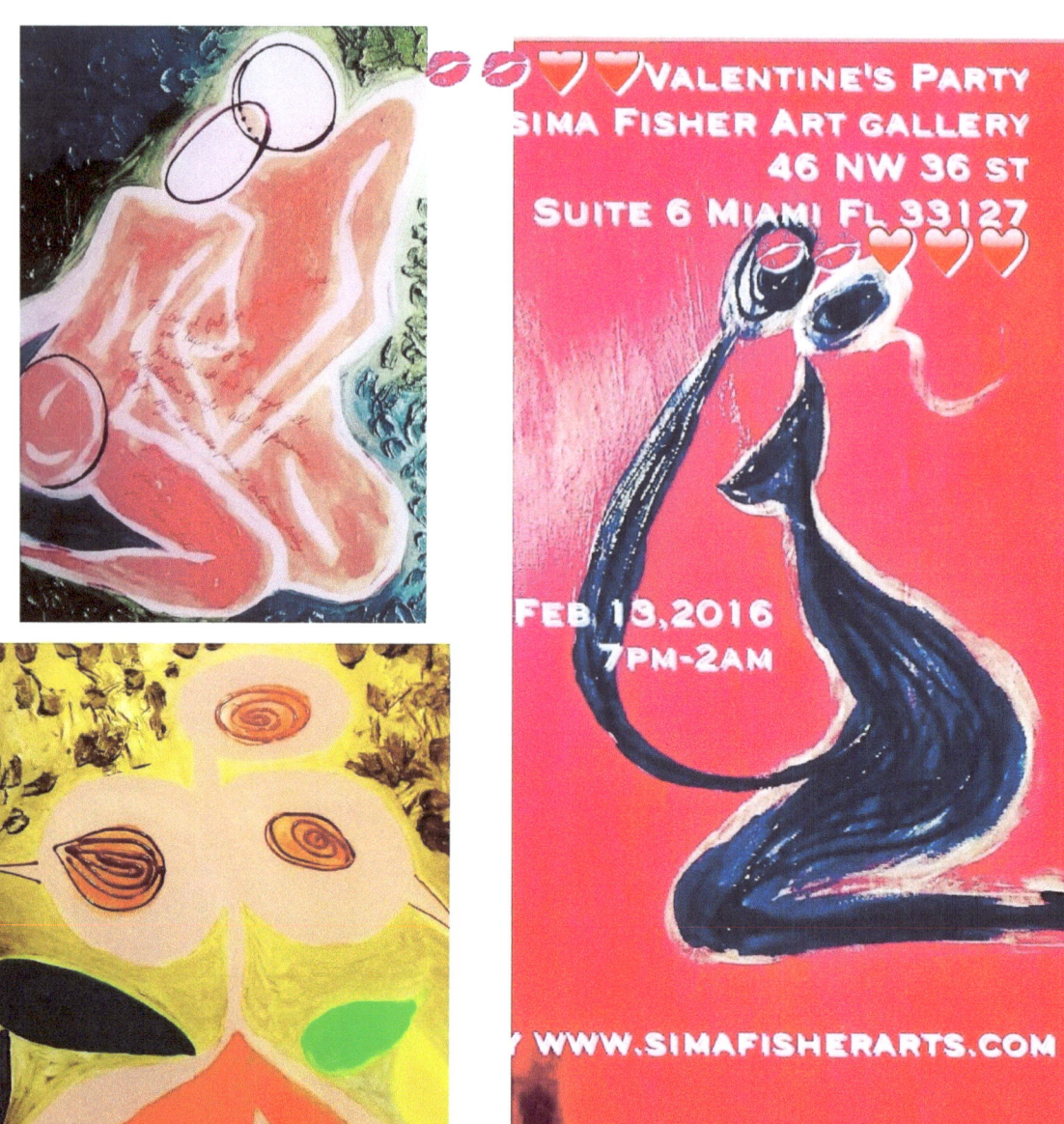

COLLABORATIONS OF LOVE-LOVE AND ART PARTIES

We love to love and we hold special parties at the gallery on a regular bases. Wine and cheese and painting parties.

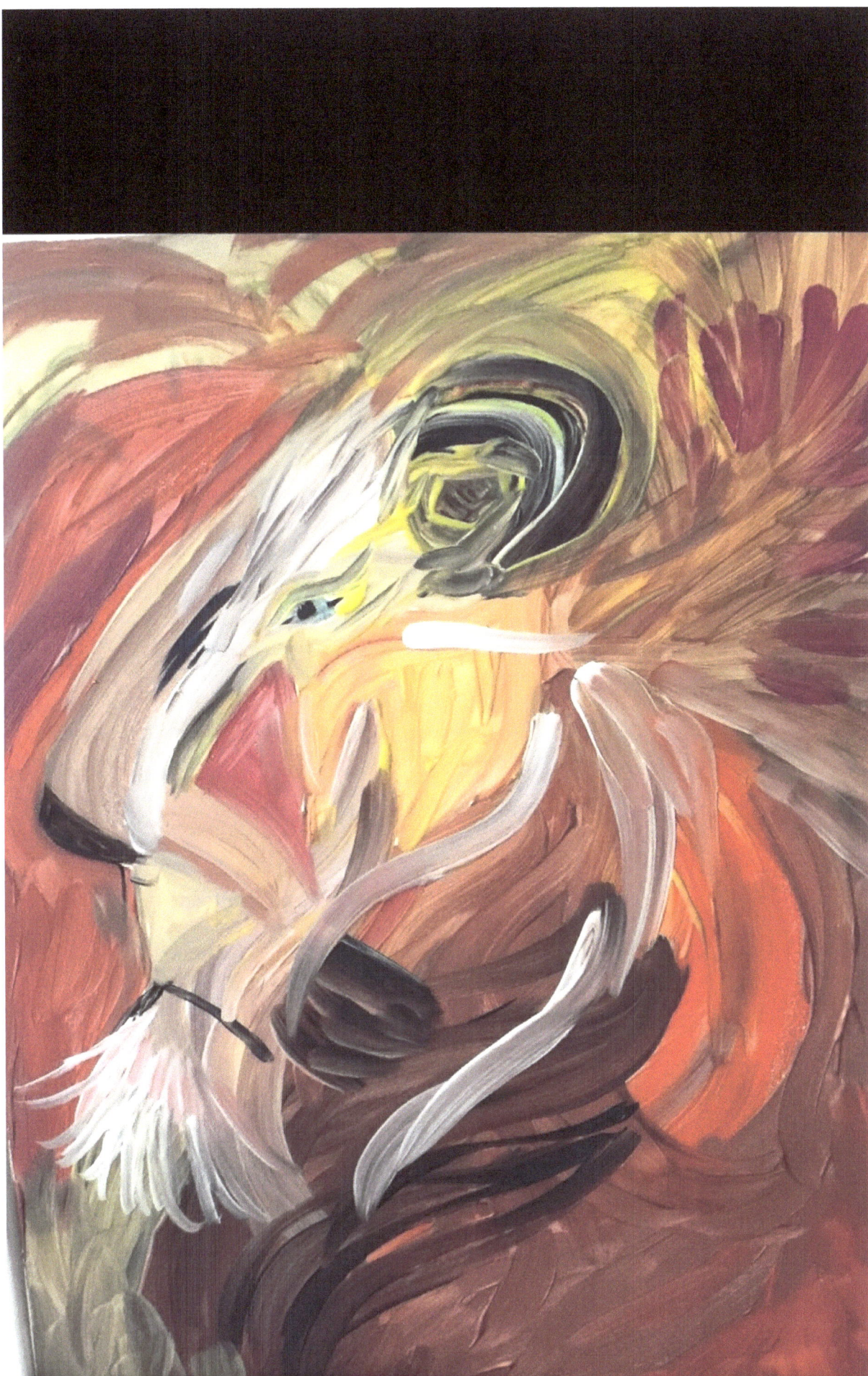

No more love (song)

I don't love him

I think I confused love with abuse

Abuse with love

Every day I cry

Every day I wonder what will help me out of it

I cry

I cry

And my little one cries too

I hide

I hide

And my little one hides too

I'm lonely

I'm torn up inside

Because he did it all on purpose

He left me stranded without you

Tears run down my cheeks

But he's not allowed to cry no more

So I cry for him

While I lay next to him

It's all I can do

Self-esteem (song)

I feel like he's the only one who will stay with

Me

I feel like he's the only one

Because he made me beg for him

Beg for the trash on the ground

When all the others put me up high

He smashes me on the floor

Then picks me off the ground and says

I don't deserve anymore

You can say what you want

You can beat me too

But don't hurt my child anymore

I won't let him become you

You musta (song)

You musta known is stop caring bout you long ago

You musta known I don't think about You

You musta known it would lead to thus

You musta know

You musta musta

You must know by all the tears that fell

You musta known by all the girls you put under your spell

You musta known

You musta known

You musta musta

If you didn't you were so blind and didn't card

You never questioned me or even stared

It was all in your ways that was so into yours so

You couldn't have

I guess I have you too much Credit

Just a big dumb guys all us girls to it

I shoulda known

That you musta not known

Dummy that I am

Giving you too much credit

That head between your legs doesn't think too much does it?

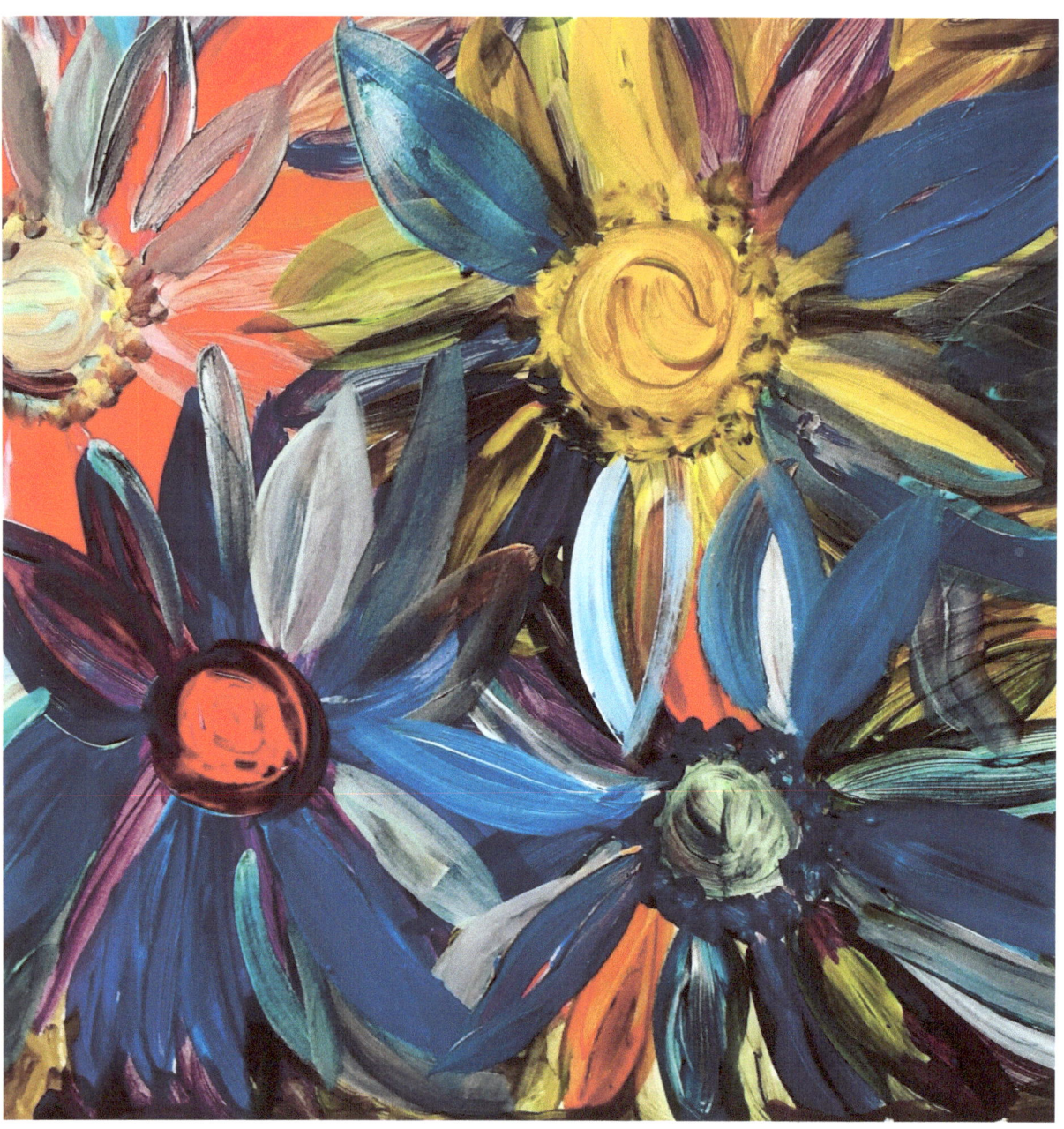

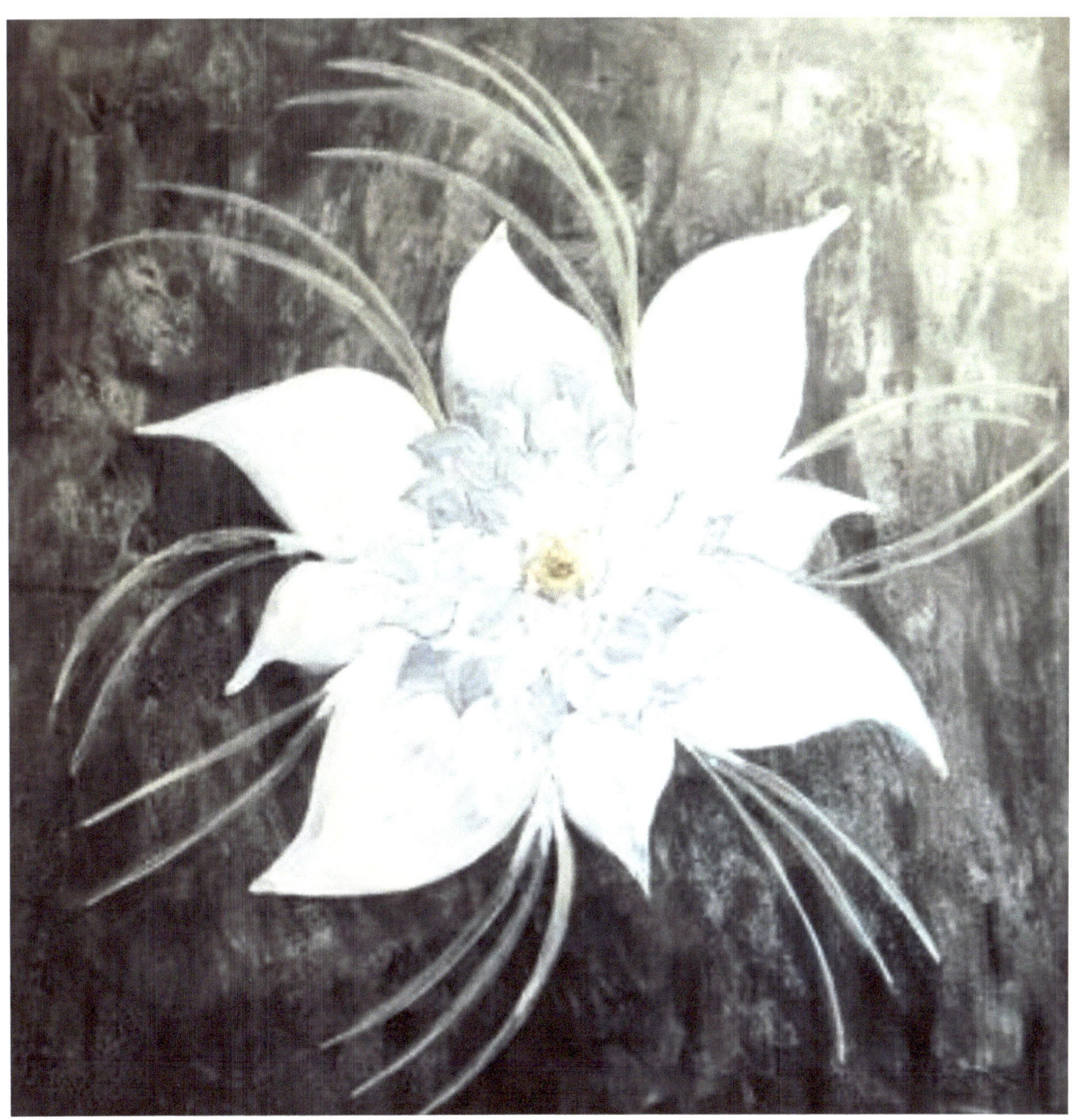

Tickles (song)

He tickles me so hard

Till I start to cry

The bruises on my back

They tell no lies

Then my child asks me

Mommy are u ok

I say no daddy hurt me and won't go away

Then he comes back around

And takes off all my clothes

And sticks it it me while I say no

I try to get away but he wants it bad

Not love and affection

Just getting him had

I have no choice but to give in

I ask him could he stop so we don't get pregnant

He wants to trap me again and again

Not because he loves me

But because he owns me

He owns me and everything I have

He owns me

He owns our child too

I'm dying every day a little at a time

All I can do is cry cry and cry more

I don't even know who I am anymore

I keep myself busy to distract myself from the pain

Because when he left me for another I felt pain too

Sometimes I wish he would find another victim again. But I realize he never will because I'm his only property